SEINSOTH

THE ROUGH-AND-TUMBLE LIFE OF A DODGER

STEVEN K. WAGNER

SUNBURY
PRESS

Mechanicsburg, PA USA

Published by Sunbury Press, Inc.
Mechanicsburg, Pennsylvania

www.sunburypress.com

For information about special discounts for bulk purchases, please contact Sunbury Press Orders Dept. at (855) 338-8359 or orders@sunburypress.com.

To request one of our authors for speaking engagements or book signings, please contact Sunbury Press Publicity Dept. at publicity@sunburypress.com.

ISBN: 978-1-62006-716-1 (Hardcover)
ISBN: 978-1-62006-717-8 (Mobipocket)

Library of Congress Control Number: 2016960211

FIRST SUNBURY PRESS EDITION: November 2016

Product of the United States of America
0 1 1 2 3 5 8 13 21 34 55

Set in Bookman Old Style
Designed by Crystal Devine
Cover by Lawrence Knorr
Edited by Janice Rhayem

Continue the Enlightenment!

For my grandmother, Frances Pawlik,
who taught me to love baseball

CONTENTS

Foreword..vii

Introduction..1

1. Born for Baseball....................................16

2. Arcadia..26

3. Hometown Hero......................................39

4. Prep Champions......................................57

5. USC Calling Card....................................65

6. Savior in Cardinal and Gold..................77

7. Breakout Season......................................91

8. NCAA Champions..................................105

9. Knockdowns and Niceties....................118

10. Dodger Blue..128

11. Pinnacle..136

12. End of the Road..................................141

Epilogue..157

Afterword..168

Acknowledgments......................................171

Appendix..175

Index..188

Works Cited..196

About the Author......................................199

*"He was a good ballplayer.
He had power, he could do everything."*

–Tommy Lasorda, former manager,
Los Angeles Dodgers

1947 – 1969 (Michael Frazier)

FOREWORD

Tommy Hutton

Tommy Hutton has been involved with professional baseball for more than fifty years—seventeen as a player and thirty-four as a broadcaster. He played twelve years in the major leagues, including two seasons with the Los Angeles Dodgers —in 1966 and 1969, the year his cousin, Bill Seinsoth, signed with the team.

As the summers pass, memories of my cousin, Bill Seinsoth, remain etched in my mind. I'm grateful for that, because in many ways Bill and his family, especially his father—my Uncle Bill—had a big impact on me as I strove to become a professional baseball player.

Bill and I were first cousins, childhood friends, students of his dad, Bill Seinsoth Sr., and, if we'd thought about it, rivals once removed, playing the same position, but at different ballparks and at different professional levels in different regions of California, although for the same organization: the Los Angeles Dodgers. Our purpose was a common one: to secure a roster spot, preferably first base, for that storied major-league ball club, one of baseball's most successful organizations and our hometown team.

When I was young my father took me to watch Uncle Bill, known affectionately as Big Bill, play baseball, knowing that I enjoyed spending time with my cousin and learning the game from firsthand observation. It was Big Bill, a longtime minor leaguer and briefly a major leaguer, who took Bill Jr. and me under his wing and taught us the fundamentals of a sport he loved and that we, in turn, also grew to love: baseball. That tutelage was never forced, but rather we appreciated receiving direction from a real baseball player who was willing to guide us along, instilling a love for the game that stuck with both of us. As often as I could, I joined in the fun that Bill Jr. certainly enjoyed with his father over many years in their own backyard.

Like many boys growing up during the 1950s, Bill and I dreamed of becoming major-league baseball players. Although my cousin remained on track to achieve that goal, his dream of becoming a big leaguer and a member of the Dodgers tragically fell short. Had he lived to fulfill the enormous potential he demonstrated at each and every level of play, I have no doubt that my cousin would have accomplished everything he envisioned when we were kids playing on the ball fields and playgrounds of Southern California. Baseball was a big part of his life, and Bill Jr. always got the most out of life.

Never mind the many bumps and bruises that came his way as he grew and matured, so often, in fact, that it must have concerned his parents. He was driven out of Little League by complaints and intimidation from those who believed he was too good. He was slashed twice across the arm in incidents that might have ended his career either in high school or college. There were serious beanings, broken noses, a broken hand, and other injuries. Finally, as if those weren't enough, an automobile accident claimed his life on the warm California desert just as he was climbing up the ladder within the Dodgers organization. Except for the fatal crash, none of those incidents could stop Bill Seinsoth. Instead, they drove him to excel with even more commitment and determination. That was typical Bill Seinsoth: take the bad, turn it into good, then go out and hit booming home runs.

My debut with the Dodgers was in 1966, and as I again played for the team three years later, Bill was following up behind me in the organization. As a first baseman/outfielder I certainly had aspirations of becoming the team's full-time first baseman, although reality told me otherwise—there were solid veterans ahead of me. Bill, a formidable challenger, had similar hopes, and as his cousin I cheered him on. He had excelled at that position for a national championship college team, was drafted twice by the Dodgers, played well during his first season with the team's minor-league affiliate in Bakersfield, California, was on his way to advancing toward a higher level of play, and seemed to be gaining traction as an up-and-coming, young ballplayer. As fate would have it, I was traded by the Dodgers after the 1971 season. Could Bill Seinsoth have become the player to eventually settle in at first base? There were—and still are—those in the organization who believe he would have.

As children growing up in the 1950s, California was the place to be. To Bill and me, baseball was king, and we chased our dream of playing professionally with all the skill we could rally. In high school, baseball was a top priority. Later on, still baseball. For both of us it was always baseball and more baseball. Bill knew what he wanted at an early age, and he sought success with a determination that was contagious. That success came in the form of hitting and pitching a baseball, and all the right people noticed. One of them was Rod Dedeaux, perhaps the greatest college coach of all time and a man who had his eye on my cousin as early as Little League. Another was Ben Wade, director of scouting for the Dodgers. With those two in his corner and a monumental swing, there was no way Bill Seinsoth would miss his calling as a major-league baseball player.

In fact, Bill never missed anything, including pitched baseballs. He was the best his Little League could muster. He was the California Interscholastic Federation's top player in high school. He was College World Series MVP and an all-American. He was the Dodgers' top draft choice. He was fourth on the Bakersfield Dodgers in home runs and fifth in RBI, despite joining the team late in the season and having far fewer at bats than players with better numbers. He achieved those numbers despite blurred vision that set in when a fastball struck him in the eye, knocking him unconscious. You could put Bill down, but never out—at least not permanently. Or so I thought.

Then came the tragic news: Bill Seinsoth, a potential superstar in the prime of life, was gone. Gone? People don't pass away at age twenty-two, I thought. Future Dodgers don't die. People with everything to live for don't just stop living—they continue on to pursue all that life has promised them.

When word of Bill's passing first came to light, my parents telephoned me at Jack Murphy Stadium in San Diego. The news of his death shocked and saddened the entire family, especially my aunt and uncle—Bill's parents—and his two sisters. However, in time, everyone continued on with their lives as best they could. They had to. The years passed—ten, twenty-five, now almost half a century. For no reason I can think of, little has been reported about Bill Seinsoth during most of that time. Until now.

This book puts in perspective the entirety of Bill's remarkable life, a life that touched many people despite its short duration. Bill was not just a great baseball player, but a complete person who faced adversity and hardship—and there was much of it—with grace, dignity, tenacity, and a broad smile. When the end came and the cards and letters from well-wishers were all put aside, one stood out above the others. It perfectly sums up the life and times of Bill Seinsoth, a life that the author explores in moving detail. It read, "One thing you know more than anyone is how much better the world is because your son passed this way. You have every reason to be proud of him . . ."

The card was signed: *Ronald Reagan.*

Bill "No-hit" Seinsoth was a young man who made the world a better place simply by the way he lived his life. He lived large, as baseball legends do. He also died large, and far too young for most people who knew and followed him

Dodger Stadium scoreboard, 1969 (*Seinsoth family photo*)

to understand and accept. Like the Dodger blue that ran through his veins, his departure left the baseball world feeling a different kind of blue—an eternal sense of sadness. This is the story of Bill Seinsoth, his extraordinarily gifted life, and what might have been.

INTRODUCTION

"You have to love the game."

–William Robert Seinsoth, baseball player

During the sixteen years that our lives overlapped, I saw Bill Seinsoth hit a pitched baseball only once. That was in 1969, just months before he was killed in a widely publicized automobile accident at the close of his first season in the Los Angeles Dodgers organization, which had pegged him as the team's first baseman of the future. On that day, track practice had ended late, and as I exited the athletic field house at Arcadia High School I perceived a commotion at the nearby ball field, where the varsity squad was practicing much like it did every afternoon as summer approached. I moved closer to observe.

There was nothing untoward, rather the moment was one of stilled amazement: players were standing around, each paying close attention as a batter I'd not seen before swatted baseballs harder, farther, and with more authority than I'd seen them hit in a long time. It was clear to anyone watching that this was no ordinary baseball player. This was a bona fide star, a blue chipper.

As I pressed close against the chain-link backstop, staring through the galvanized mesh toward home plate, the larger-than-life figure drilled pitch after pitch over the right field fence and onto Duarte Road, a main thoroughfare that runs through Arcadia, California, from east to west. The scene was a bit improbable. You could count on one hand, or perhaps one finger, the number of players who had graduated from Arcadia High School with that kind of ability, so this must be someone special, I figured. From a distance I didn't recognize the face, but I soon found out it *was* someone special. Someone very special.

"Who is *that*?" I asked, stopping a friend who was walking past Giambrone Field as the late afternoon sun hung just above the administration building. I pointed toward the batter's box as the Gehrigian slugger wearing Trojan flannels dug his cleats into the dirt, unconcerned with the fading light of day. He fixed his eyes straight ahead as his former high school coach, standing sixty feet and six inches in front of him, broke into a windup and fired: BAM—a ball exploded off his bat, soared over the right-centerfield fence, and bounced toward the Arcadia Public Library nearly a tenth of a mile away.

"Bill Seinsoth."

Seinsoth, I repeated to myself. Almost everyone knew Bill Seinsoth, I thought, or at least knew something about him: California Interscholastic Federation (CIF) Player of the Year in 1965 as a fireballing, left-handed pitcher for CIF champion Arcadia High School. College World Series Most Outstanding Player as a hard-hitting first baseman on USC's 1968 national championship team. Drafted by the Los Angeles Dodgers (twice), Houston Astros, Baltimore Orioles, and Washington Senators. At the time of his death he was the leading candidate to replace slick-fielding Wes Parker as first-baseman for the Dodgers. Seinsoth was, many believed, one of the finest prospects ever to come out of California. Or anywhere.

"He was definitely a professional prospect," former Dodger Tommy Hutton, a cousin of Seinsoth, said in an interview many years later. "He had all the tools" (Wagner 1991).

Since he first dominated Arcadia National Little League hitters in the late 1950s, headlines and box scores in the local *Arcadia Tribune* had promised a bright future for the muscular, hard-hitting Seinsoth. That spring afternoon in 1969 I saw for myself what headlines, box scores, and

With his hopes high and a look of confidence on his face, Seinsoth works out with the major-league Dodgers shortly before his death in 1969

weekly sports columns could only intimate: William Robert Seinsoth, whose visit that afternoon to his high school alma mater would be his final one, was for real.

As a ballplayer and as an individual, Bill Seinsoth had it all. The only son of a journeyman minor-league pitcher who advanced briefly to the St. Louis Browns' major-league roster, he certainly had the right pedigree. At six foot two, 220 pounds—bigger than Babe Ruth, but without the wide girth—Seinsoth had a major-league physique, and his muscular stature enabled him to translate his picture-perfect swing into booming home runs. His sturdy build surprised no one, least of all his mother, as at birth Seinsoth had weighed a whopping nine pounds, thirteen ounces—more than ample for the future star on an NCAA championship baseball team.

Seinsoth's broad smile, blonde hair, and box-office looks were also striking, prompting younger sister, Dauna, to once remark, "All the girls wanted autographed pictures of Bill, so I would sign his name and sell them for fifty cents. He was in *such* demand." Throughout high school Dauna, now Dauna Frazier, served as her brother's unofficial publicity manager. "I was so close to him—all of *his* friends were *my* friends" (Wagner 1991).

Others agreed with Dauna's assessment that her brother had star power, especially with the girls. As hometown columnist Bill DeMuth was calling Seinsoth "one of the most handsome athletes around" (DeMuth 1967), reporter Vickie Garcia, in a lighthearted story for the USC *Daily Trojan*, was echoing that compliment:

> **Where do the athletes find their women? Sometimes, they don't. The girls find them or go after them, as the case may be. For proof, go to a Trojan baseball game and count the number of coeds who sigh when Bill Seinsoth steps up to the plate (Garcia 1969).**

What's more, he was genial, easygoing—everyone liked Bill Seinsoth. Except, perhaps, the assailant who sliced his arm for no apparent reason halfway through his phenomenal prep career. Or the attacker who lacerated him with a knife in a tense altercation at a restaurant near the USC campus, where Seinsoth was well known.

Yes, Bill Seinsoth had everything—including a name that screamed power. Seinsoth. *SEINSOTH!* Then, in the blink of an eye, in a cruel burst of wind and the crumpling crush of metal against pavement, his car overturned on a wind-blown stretch of California highway believed to be the deadliest in the US (Hargrove 2010). In a flash, the baseball wunderkind had nothing—not even life.

In a weird sense, Seinsoth's very name may have been his undoing. When his car rolled over on a lonely stretch of Interstate 15 near the desert ghost town Calico, it was speculated that a carton of custom-made Louisville Slugger bats with his name blazoned on the smooth, tan barrels may have struck him in the head as the car flipped onto the warm asphalt, delivering the blow that ultimately proved fatal. The bats, a gift for a friend, were identical to those he hoped would carry him from the Class-A Bakersfield Dodgers to perhaps a short stint in Double-A ball, then on to Triple-A, and eventually to the Los Angeles Dodgers, a team that had drafted him twice during the preceding years—most recently in the first round—and coveted him as its first baseman of the future. With Parker in the twilight of his career, Seinsoth was pegged as the man who would carry his mantle on the right corner of the infield for at least the next decade—perhaps even longer. In the Dodgers' mind there was no one in the organization better—not Steve Garvey, not cousin Hutton, who at that time was a utility first baseman for the Dodgers, not anyone. Bill Seinsoth was the man of the moment—but the moment was fleeting.

"I have no doubt Bill Seinsoth would have been the Dodger first baseman for a long time to come," Rod Dedeaux, the late USC coach who converted the pitcher-first baseman to a full-time first baseman, once said (Wagner 1991). If anyone could evaluate baseball talent, it was Dedeaux. The coach of eleven NCAA championship teams during his forty-five years at the helm of USC, he is widely regarded as the greatest college baseball coach of all time.

Ironically, on September 1, 1969, just five days before Seinsoth's tragic automobile accident, Garvey made his major-league debut for the Dodgers, going 0 for 1 as a pinch hitter in a 10-6 win over the New York Mets. On September 10, three days after Seinsoth died and three days before the funeral, Garvey collected his first major-league hit in another impromptu plate appearance,

drilling a shot to left field off Denny Lemaster of the
Houston Astros; the single would be his only hit that
season. It was around September 7 when Garvey's wife,
Cyndy, overheard a Dodger teammate's curious remark
after the player apparently learned about Seinsoth's
automobile accident, which stunned the populace from
Arcadia north to Bakersfield and throughout the Los
Angeles metropolitan area and all of Southern California:
"Steve Garvey just got a big break," she quoted the player
as saying (Wagner 1991). Twenty-two years later, after a
prominent newspaper ran an article on Seinsoth's
staggeringly successful career and tragically short life,
she telephoned the author to say that after all those years
the unidentified player's remark finally made sense to
her: Garvey's "big break," she believed, was the crash that
took Seinsoth's life, leaving the Dodgers scrambling for a
replacement who could field with grace while hitting home
runs with equivalent ferocity. That replacement,
eventually, was Garvey, who continued on to compile
near-Hall-of-Fame numbers during the fourteen years he
was with the Dodgers and his nineteen years overall as a
major-league first baseman.

Since it opened in 1952, Arcadia High School, which is
nestled at the foot of the San Gabriel Mountains just east
of Pasadena, has captured the coveted CIF baseball crown
just once—in 1965 when Seinsoth was a senior. In its
own long and colorful baseball history, USC has won
twelve NCAA titles, eleven of them orchestrated by
Dedeaux. The 1968 team, led by junior sensation
Seinsoth, began a string of six titles in seven years and
ushered in a period of dominance never before seen in
college baseball. Had he lived long enough to play for the
Dodgers, there is reason to believe that team's success
would have reflected the limitless skills of its likely first
baseman. He was, simply, a winner no matter whom he
played for or at what level.

During his three years at Arcadia High the varsity baseball team won its only CIF title after losing in the finals the previous season. While at USC, after winning a national title in 1968, his team failed to earn a berth in the College World Series the following year, in part due to a serious beaning suffered by Seinsoth; after he graduated, USC won the next five NCAA championships. In 1970, the year after his death—and perhaps motivated by it—the Bakersfield Dodgers won their first California League championship. As a player, Seinsoth brought home championships, and when he wasn't there to win them, he inspired teams by his absence.

Certainly, major-league baseball has never been immune to off-field tragedy—many players and managers, some of them standouts, have been felled by accident and injury through the years. On August 2, 1979, New York Yankees catcher Thurman Munson, a former American League MVP and seven-time all-star, died when the light plane he was using to practice takeoffs and landings crashed at Akron-Canton Airport in Ohio. On Christmas day 1989 frequent Yankees manager Billy Martin was killed when the pickup truck he was riding in plunged down a 300-foot embankment near Binghamton, New York. And on March 23, 1993, Tim Crews and Steve Olin of the Cleveland Indians met a similar fate when the motorboat Crews was piloting struck a dock at high speed. The list goes on to include Lymon Bostock, California Angels, murdered; former National League MVP Roberto Clemente, Pittsburgh Pirates, airplane crash; and Ray Chapman of the Cleveland Indians, who is perhaps the best known of all big leaguers to have lost their lives tragically. Chapman, who died in 1920, is the only player in the history of major-league baseball to have been killed by a pitched ball, something Seinsoth may have recollected after a delivery from Oregon State pitcher Lloyd Wilson struck him above the right eye during a game against the Beavers on April 21, 1969. Some have speculated that the after-effects of the beaning may have played a role in the crash that took his life.

While tragic accidents do happen, rarely do they extinguish the life of a player with such significant potential as Seinsoth had. Rarely do they involve athletes as beloved as he was. And rarely does the death of a ballplayer leave so many people scratching their heads in disbelief, trying to reconcile the loss of such a popular and likable player just as his star was beginning to rise. No community felt the loss more keenly than Arcadia.

As a young boy I grew up reading about Seinsoth's baseball exploits—there were many of them—in the local twice-weekly newspaper. We never met, although as children and later on as adolescents we were practically neighbors. He lived on Santa Anita Avenue just down the street from the Bud Lyndon Swim School, and I was reared on Altern Street only a short walk from Chicken Delight. We played on the same Little League team—sponsored by the 7-Up Bottling Co.—although he for the last time in 1958 and I for the first time in 1963. Our homes were situated on either side of Richard Henry Dana Jr. Junior High School, which we both attended, and as I studied in class or played various sports on the school's sprawling field, I might have caught a glimpse of him returning home after baseball or basketball practice during his high school years. We also had attended Camino Grove and Santa Anita elementary schools, and both of us participated in the Arcadia Babe Ruth League. Our families attended Arcadia Presbyterian Church. Later, I played on the same basketball court at Arcadia High School where Seinsoth first turned heads as a prep athlete in 1962. We also played under the same basketball coach, Vallie Robinson, who was an assistant during the Seinsoth years and had risen to head coach by the time I arrived at the school. Seinsoth and I trod similar paths as we grew up in Arcadia, however, those paths never seemed to intersect.

From 1962, his first year as a high school student-athlete, until his death in 1969 the *Arcadia Tribune* couldn't get enough of Bill Seinsoth, nor could its readers. In time, his name became a fixture on its sports pages every Thursday and Sunday over the course of those seven years, three of them while he attended Arcadia High and four spent at USC. Looking back, he clearly was a favorite of local sportswriters Mannie Pineda, Bill DeMuth, and Fred Robledo. Then, with his sudden death on September 7, 1969, the proliferation of stories trailed off. There was occasional mention of him for a few years afterward as memorials were offered—within days of his passing, a scholarship, the Bill Seinsoth Memorial Scholarship Award, was established at USC; four years later the Bill Seinsoth Award also was created at USC to recognize the player with the highest batting average. In 1970 Arcadia High announced that its player of the year award henceforth would be called, simply, the Bill Seinsoth Memorial Award, with a plaque depicting the ballplayer still affixed inside the gymnasium where he starred for the varsity basketball team. Now among the oldest and most coveted awards that an athlete at the school can receive, it honors, as the permanent plaque reads, an exemplary player's "outstanding contribution to self, school, community and others"—qualities he personified (Bill Seinsoth Memorial Award 2015). Finally, to honor his son's memory, Seinsoth's father even threw out the first pitch before an Alaska Goldpanners game in Fairbanks, where his son had played for three seasons as a member of that legendary squad of college baseball players. As news of his death began to sink in, however, the articles and memorials eventually stopped. At last, Bill Seinsoth had been put to rest. It was time for life to continue.

Somehow, that didn't seem good enough, and I made an attempt to rekindle Seinsoth's fading memory in 1991, writing an extensive article for the *Los Angeles Times*. The *Times* gave it a lengthy, complex headline, perhaps reflecting the reality that Seinsoth never did anything the easy way: *They're Left to Wonder What Might Have Been: Friends and Family of Arcadia's Seinsoth Recall the Talent that Seemed Destined for Glory in Dodger Blue.* If nothing else, the story prompted Cyndy Garvey to reveal the comment she overheard in the Dodgers clubhouse shortly after Seinsoth's death, the one that may have intimated Steve Garvey's bright future as a Los Angeles Dodger.

So why write a book, and why now—forty-five years after the death of Seinsoth, who had become well known on the national collegiate stage, but certainly not in the professional baseball arena? Why make ado about a man who never played in a single major-league ballgame, a player whose bat was silenced after one promising season in the low minor leagues? It's simple. The trickle of stories after his death on September 7, 1969, and the in-depth piece written a quarter-century ago failed to capture the essence of Bill Seinsoth: his magnanimous persona, the hope unfulfilled, the deep disappointment and overwhelming grief felt by many when he passed away, the affection that was silenced when two bats were crossed and laid atop his chest, bats and balls placed next to him in the coffin before Seinsoth was laid in the ground at Rose Hills Memorial Park and Mortuary—Acacia Lawn, section seven, lot 3090, grave three—and how life eventually continued on without him. It's hard to imagine, fans and teammates must have thought, a world without Bill Seinsoth, who epitomized both life and baseball with his youthful exuberance and gritty determination.

Years after his son's untimely death, Seinsoth's father was hired as equipment manager at Arcadia High School. One day in 1984, while raking the pitching mound where his son so often mesmerized opposing batters as a prep star, Big Bill suffered a massive heart attack and died hours later. Fourteen years later Seinsoth's mother, Jane, passed away at the age of seventy-nine. A sister, Janice, took ill and died at age sixty-eight in 2009. Only younger sister, Dauna, survives. Somehow, it seems an appropriate time to discuss in detail the life and extraordinarily exciting times of Bill Seinsoth, who but for an unthinkable moment would have served as a fitting proxy in fulfilling his father's long-ago dream to play in the major leagues.

I began my research by calling the Alaska Goldpanners, where Seinsoth enjoyed three wonderfully satisfying summers of baseball. Todd Dennis, who rose through the ranks from hot dog vender to batboy to general manager, answered that call. When I told him I was interested in writing a book about a man who played with the team many years earlier and who had died in an automobile accident, Dennis, who has been associated with the team for thirty-five of his years, exclaimed, matter-of-factly, "Bill Seinsoth." He then added, "I never actually saw him play, but he's probably my favorite Goldpanner of all time." Therein lies the essence of Bill Seinsoth: after all the years that have passed since his death, Seinsoth's success, personality, and charisma somehow were able to transcend time itself to charm people such as Dennis, who never saw him play an inning of baseball.

It's easier to appreciate other Goldpanners, those who went on to enjoy long and productive major-league careers and who are not as far removed as Seinsoth from the daily spotlight. Players like Hall of Famer Tom Seaver, a member of the 1964 Goldpanner squad and winner of 311 games in his major-league career; slugger Dave Kingman, who played with the team during the summer that Seinsoth died and ended up hitting 442 major-league home runs; and Bob Boone, a teammate during all three of Seinsoth's Goldpanner seasons. According to Dennis, Seinsoth and Boone maintained a friendly, competitive camaraderie throughout their Goldpanner years, with Boone winning team MVP honors in 1966 and 1968 and Seinsoth capturing the award in 1967. Boone went on to play nineteen seasons in the major leagues, making the National League all-star team three times and the American League squad once.

With his ability to hit for power and his stellar glove, Seinsoth, like Boone, was a formidable ballplayer. However, whether he eventually may have proven himself the better all-around major-league player is open to conjecture. The only available comparison involves the years that Boone and Seinsoth spent together in Fairbanks, and during those three seasons, Boone had the edge.

Which brings us back to this book. Since the *Times* article on Seinsoth first appeared, many of the sources who were interviewed have departed. Seinsoth's mother has passed away, and gone, too, are Dedeaux and Seinsoth's high school coach, Lani Exton. Ben Wade, who retired as director of scouting for the Dodgers in 1991 and was instrumental in bringing Seinsoth to the organization, has also died. Time is fleeting, and the legion of players who either played with or recall Seinsoth diminishes with each passing spring. No matter—others remain to speak on his behalf, people like Dedeaux's son, Justin, who began assisting with the USC baseball program after his short minor-league career ended in 1966 and worked as an assistant coach under his father beginning in Seinsoth's first varsity season and continuing through 1978—an eleven-year period that encompassed eight national championships. Many teammates also remain, including Jay Jaffe, center fielder on the 1968 national championship team and a successful criminal attorney in Beverly Hills, California; Tom House, a former major leaguer whose wedding party included Seinsoth; and ex-big leaguers Bill "Spaceman" Lee, Jim Barr, and Mike Adamson.

To fully appreciate Seinsoth and his accomplishments, it's important to put his record in context. One way to do that is to stand him alongside others from the high school where it all began, those who went on to play professional baseball. In the sixty-four-year history of Arcadia High School's athletic program a number of players have gone on to enjoy big-league careers. Perhaps most notable is Bruce Bochte, whose skill level approached Seinsoth's when he joined the baseball team the year after its big left-hander graduated. Bochte played thirteen seasons in the major leagues, making the American League all-star team in 1979.

Steve Kemp, who attended USC after Seinsoth and was a first-round draft pick, played eleven seasons in the major leagues. He played alongside Bochte in the 1979 American League all-star game and was named to the squad again in 1981. Like Seinsoth, a ball struck him in the eye, ending his career.

Chris Arnold, a Little League and high school teammate of Seinsoth, played six seasons with the San Francisco Giants, retiring with a lifetime batting average of .237. Also playing for the Giants was Pat Larkin, whose career was limited to ten innings pitched during a single season: 1983.

Dave Hostetler, another product of USC, played five seasons with three ball clubs, retiring in 1988 with thirty-seven home runs and 124 RBI. Posting similar numbers was Mark Smith, who played eight seasons with five clubs and notched thirty-two homers and 130 RBI before retiring from the game in 2003.

Many others played at various minor-league levels, not efficiently enough to advance to the big leagues. Included are Mike Larkin (brother of Pat), who was drafted by the Kansas City Royals and played three seasons, compiling a 1.58 earned run average and advancing to Double-A twice; Neil Rasmussen, who was picked in the first round and twelfth overall by the Houston Astros in the 1971 amateur draft and advanced to Double-A before retiring; John D'Auria and Dan Blood, two seasons of Single-A ball each; Rob Mayhew, one season of Single-A ball in the Minnesota Twins organization; and Tony Torres, who the *Tribune* hailed as a future star on par with Seinsoth. Torres played one season of baseball in an independent league.

Compared to his Arcadia brethren of ballplayers, Seinsoth's tenure as a professional baseball player was among the shortest of all. However, it was also the most important in the sense that he became the yardstick by which all Arcadians are now measured. He also became a standard for success at USC, as only six other players in the history of the school—and no other first basemen—achieved the distinction of being named College World Series Most Outstanding Player; none reached the major leagues, although Seinsoth was considered a lock to ascend after he was selected eighth overall in the 1969 amateur draft. Only fourteen Trojans in the fifty-year history of the amateur draft have been chosen higher than Seinsoth in the first round, and his selection in the draft for five consecutive years—in a higher round each year, including twice in 1969—is a mark exceeded by only an elite few ballplayers.

As I began to work on this book, Ken Miller, an all-America first baseman for Dedeaux's 1959 team, described Seinsoth's legacy as a Trojan in unmistakable terms. "Bill Seinsoth was a great Trojan," he said (Wagner 2015).

Sandy Gilchrist, a two-time Olympic swimmer who knew Seinsoth during their USC days, offered further encouragement. "I was always a big fan of Bill's," he said. "I really hope the book becomes a reality" (Wagner 2015).

Perhaps Rod Dedeaux, however, said it best, projecting far beyond Seinsoth's impact as a Trojan: "I think he had the makings of a superstar," he once said (Wagner 1991).

Superstar. It's a word that is seldom used, except in the context of outstanding professional athletes—the best of the best. Built like Seinsoth, Lou Gehrig, also a first baseman, was a superstar. So was first baseman Mark McGwire, another product of USC. No matter how good McGwire was or would become, he would not bump Seinsoth from Dedeaux's all-time, all-USC team.

"Bill Seinsoth would make any team I could ever coach," Dedeaux said in 1991, four years after McGwire hit forty-nine home runs and drove in 118 RBI for the Oakland Athletics (Wagner 1991). Period.

Any team, in the mind of baseball's Coach of the Century. No matter how good the other players he coached might have been, Seinsoth would always have a place on Dedeaux's all-time, all-USC team by virtue of his ability, attitude, and smarts—he simply had it all: strong bat, outstanding glove, charisma, personality, humility, good looks, and, perhaps above all, confidence. With that in mind, here is the story of that remarkable young player, who was dealt a fatal blow long before his life should have ended. It's the story of a can't-miss star who *did* miss achieving major-league stardom due to fateful circumstances. And, while he missed playing in the major leagues, in the larger picture, life missed out on Bill Seinsoth and all that he had to offer. Nearly half a century later, Seinsoth, whom ex-teammate Jaffe described as "just a winner," is still missed by his family, friends, and teammates (Wagner 1991). This is the story of a consummate baseball player, perhaps the greatest player who never appeared in a major-league game, but someone who may have become one of baseball's brightest stars—a true winner. This is the story of Bill Seinsoth. —*SKW*

1

BORN FOR BASEBALL

*"I was never in Cub Scouts . . . I just played baseball.
That was everything . . ."*
–Bill Seinsoth, baseball player

The plain, green fence stretched from foul pole to foul pole
and was chest high to those of us Little Leaguers who
were tall for our age. By virtue of its verdant hue, it
resembled Fenway Park's Green Monster, but was far
smaller in scale. I can still remember the field
dimensions: 182 feet down both lines, 200 feet to dead
center. To a young boy, center field seemed cavernous,
much like the old Polo Grounds, but once in a while
someone cleared the fence with a monumental blast that
would elicit conversation for days, at least until another
slate of games came into view for the following Thursday
or Saturday. Although records from that period are gone
forever, Bill Seinsoth cleared the fence often during his
Little League years—perhaps more frequently than
anyone in league history. Pitching, however, was the boy's
real strength, at least early on.

Just beyond the left field fence stood a small
scoreboard where someone, usually a player or two whose
games had already been completed, hung white numbers
on hooks each time a runner scored or an out was
recorded, a hand-turned operation similar to that at
Wrigley Field. As remuneration for keeping score, kids

were rewarded with a snow cone topped with one of several flavored syrups—grape and cherry were the overwhelming favorites. Yes, Longden Field in Arcadia was a little bit Fenway, little bit Wrigley, little bit Polo Grounds. That's where *he* played, at least for a while— until he got too good and the threats and intimidation began.

The fence and scoreboard aside, there was much more to Longden Field, which the Arcadia National Little League still calls home. Like the quaint snack shack, where ice-cold snow cones and an assortment of candies and other delectables could be purchased for small change. Two wood bleachers— one for the home team and one for the visitors—were set between the snack shack and playing field, where teams congregated in narrow dugouts

As a Little Leaguer young Bill Jr. already displayed the formidable stance that would someday make him a slugger (*Seinsoth family photo*)

that seemed big-league at the time, but really weren't: wood splinters encroaching through our flannel knickers were always a threat. Based upon each boy's ability, which was demonstrated during the highly anticipated Little League tryout, players were apportioned to major- and minor-league teams whose names rolled off the tongue for many years afterward. I can still remember some of them, although most of the sponsors long ago shuttered their doors and disappeared from local commerce: Power Thrust Gasoline, Hardings Gardenland, Crown Heating, Dairyland Farms, Superior Concrete, and Arcadia Floor Covering were just a few. Arcadia Sporting Goods, owned by congenial Fred Wheeler and for many years the favored merchant of all things athletic, also sponsored a team, but hardly anyone remembers that—the store closed its doors decades ago.

At an early age the future first baseman was beginning to show his acumen around the bag, c. 1958 (*Seinsoth family photo*)

The backdrop to everything was neighboring Plymouth Elementary School, whose expansive dirt playground seemed a miniature version of the Bonneville Salt Flats and stretched for acres. For some never-explained reason, I wasn't supposed to play at Plymouth. Perhaps my parents figured that if allowed to roam there I'd get lost on the massive, brown terrain, and at that time there were no global positioning systems to reel me back in.

To boys growing up in the 1950s, as Bill Seinsoth did, Longden Field was home away from home. We practiced there once a week, sometimes twice. We played our games there on Thursday evenings and Saturday mornings. And when practicing or competing in games, we watched our friends practice and compete in *their* games. Even boys who weren't very good played Little League baseball. That was what you did. It was expected, and few strayed far from that expectation.

If you lived near Longden Field, your life was measurably easier, largely because you could come and go without the need for a parent to drive you to the ballpark. Bicycles were the preferred mode of transportation, and without bikes you simply walked. Seinsoth was a lucky one. His family's first home, on Tenth Avenue near Camino Grove Elementary School, was only a mile and a half from the ballpark, so the back and forth was easy. After that, nothing was easy. Well, throwing a baseball past batters was easy. So was hitting for distance. The rest was difficult and oftentimes painful, both physically and emotionally.

On Friday April 4, 1947, Bill Seinsoth entered a fast-changing world that would challenge him at every step along the way. He was born an early baby boomer at White Memorial Hospital in Los Angeles, weighing in at nearly ten pounds. If size alone were a determiner, he was definitely baseball material. From that day through the rest of his life his physical presence would transcend that of most other boys his age, and by the time he died, his emotional maturity had surpassed that of his peers. As his late high school coach Lani Exton put it more than two decades after Seinsoth's death, he was an adult playing with adolescents (Wagner 1991). In high school and college, the adult usually predominated, at least when it came to baseball.

Looking back, his birth venue—White Memorial Hospital—seems an appropriate one for a future major-league baseball player. Just fifteen years later, almost to the day, Dodger Stadium would open for business less than three miles from the hospital. Who would guess the blockbuster impacts that both White Memorial and later on Dodger Stadium, which were situated only a short seven-minute drive from each other, would potentially have on the future of one of baseball's most glorious sports franchises: the Los Angeles Dodgers.

Seinsoth's life took a decidedly baseball path almost from the get-go. His father, who by 1947 was a decade into a minor-league baseball career that would span a remarkable fourteen years by the time it was over, was a career ballplayer and well connected, and those connections would pay big dividends when it came time for his son to begin thinking about college. One of those connections was Rod Dedeaux, who won his first NCAA baseball championship the year after Seinsoth was born. Little did Dedeaux know that twenty-one years later

Seinsoth would guide him toward another title. He was, simply, a chip off a much larger block. That block was his father.

William Welty Seinsoth, known as Bill Sr., despite having a different middle name than his son, was born in Salt Lake City, Utah, on February 5, 1918. Like his son eventually would become, he was large in stature, and his vital statistics were listed at six foot three, 225 pounds— he was even more formidable and imposing than his talented son when the boy later peaked as a Trojan at six foot two and 220 pounds.

Bill Sr. entered professional baseball in 1936 at the youthful age of eighteen, joining the Double-A Sacramento Solons of the Pacific Coast League.

"His father and mother didn't even know he played baseball until he came home with a contract for them to sign," said his wife Jane—Bill Jr.'s mother—years later (Wagner 1991).

His debut at that level had to please the big left-handed pitcher, as he sidestepped the usual entry point for young players, the equivalent of Single-A ball or even lower, and went straight to the more advanced level. The decision may have been a regrettable one, both for Seinsoth and for St. Louis Cardinals management. Bill Sr. threw unimpressively during his first season with the Solons, appearing in thirty-four games; he won only three, lost eight, and allowed just under six runs per nine innings pitched. Clearly, there was work to be done if the hulking lefty was ever to move forward as a professional baseball player.

After that baptism his trek through the minor leagues looked very much like a bowl of alphabet soup. He began the 1937 season with Columbus Red Birds in "B" ball, going 15-7 with a 2.74 ERA, and appeared to be on an expedited track for success; those numbers were good enough to earn him a return ticket to Double-A later that season, again with his first team the Solons, where he only pitched a total of six innings and earned no decisions. After that his numbers were consistently decent: 10-11 with a 3.36 ERA pitching for three teams in 1938, including the Double-A Rochester Red Wings and Columbus; 17-10 with a 2.41 ERA in 1939 pitching for Columbus of the South Atlantic League, Class-B ball; and 16-11 with a 3.39 ERA pitching for two teams in 1940, including Double-A Rochester toward the end of the season. His best season was in 1942 when he won twenty-four games in thirty-four decisions and recorded a sterling 2.79 ERA in 300 innings for the Single-A New Orleans Pelicans of the Southern Association. After posting a remarkable two dozen wins in his seventh season of pro ball, Bill Sr. again was elevated to the Double-A level, going 9-15 with a 3.40 ERA for the Toledo Mud Hens in 1943.

In 1938, Bill Sr. kneels in front of Walt Alston, who later managed Big Bill's nephew Tommy Hutton on the Los Angeles Dodgers

After remaining with Double-A Toledo for the entire 1944 season, where he was 16-11 with an acceptable 4.08 ERA, the St. Louis Browns, a fixture in the American League since 1902 and a fixture as losers, called him up to the big club. The team, which had acquired him the previous year, went on to win its only pennant in the franchise's history that season, however, Bill Sr. was merely an observer of the team's fortunes. He remained on the bench during his short stay with the Luke Sewell-managed Browns and failed to enter a single big-league game. At that point the handwriting was on the wall: his one and only chance at achieving every boy's dream—playing in a major-league baseball game—had come and gone with the speed of a Bill Sr. fastball.

Bill Sr. is a formidable figure as a member of the Toledo Mud Hens, c.1943

The elder Seinsoth was drafted into the armed forces the following year and missed the entire 1945 season, pitching only sparingly in a brief stint with Triple-A Sacramento in 1946. Although his earned run average was excellent in 1947, his last season in Double-A ball, as well as in 1949 and 1950—3.17, 2.80, and 2.44; he never earned another position on a major-league roster. That may have pleased opponents who rejected his occasional high dudgeon antics.

According to a news account from 1947, the elder Seinsoth was involved in a Fourth of July fracas with Stan Benjamin, a Houston minor leaguer. After Houston scored five runs in a raucous second inning, the fireworks began when Seinsoth heaved the ball out of the ballpark in disgust. His next pitch then struck Benjamin, who threw his bat at the pitcher.

> **The two met halfway between the plate and the mound. They were not separated until action had shifted over to the first base line.**
>
> **The entire squads of both San Antonio and Houston, plus a flock of policemen, moved in to separate the two players. Neither was injured in the scuffle, but both were promptly heaved out of the game . . .**
>
> **The antics of Seinsoth and Benjamin highlighted an otherwise drab game . . . (Punches Fly in Texas Circuit 1947)**

His career, obviously, was anything but drab. Bill Sr. left baseball three years later in 1950 with an overall record of 156-130 and a lifetime-earned run average of 3.22—excellent numbers for a journeyman pitcher at any level. He continued to play semipro ball for more than a decade, well after his son had begun to make his mark as a young ballplayer in the 1960s.

It is not known why Seinsoth, who continued to post solid numbers almost every year, including his final season, never caught on with a big-league club and continued to bounce up and down between various minor-league levels. Add to that his ability to hit for both average and power—as a pitcher in 1939 he hit .298 with two home runs and seventeen RBI—and he appeared to be a legitimate major-league prospect: in thirteen seasons he hit .254 with sixty-two doubles, twelve triples, and thirty-one home runs—not bad for a pitcher, although to his credit he was built like Babe Ruth. A wire service reporter portrayed his ability to hit and pitch in a 1938 dispatch, noting that Seinsoth doubled in the ninth inning of a game to provide the winning run after pitching four scoreless innings in relief to secure the win.

Former New York Yankees outfielder/first baseman Irv Noren, who spent four seasons in the minor leagues, eleven seasons in the majors, and knew both Bill Sr. and Bill Jr., theorized why ballplayers from that bygone era, such as Seinsoth Sr., spent their entire careers at baseball's lower echelon, known as the bush leagues. In Bill Sr.'s case, he played minor-league baseball until he was in his forties.

"There weren't seventy-five [major-league] teams like there are today," Noren said sarcastically. "There are guys in the big leagues now who should be in the minor leagues. [They] call players up from Triple-A and Double-A who are 3-7 and they start them [in a major-league game]" (Wagner 2015).

Bill Sr., a former Army artillery sergeant who was accidentally shot in the pitching hand by a fellow soldier, perhaps speeding his exit from baseball, was better than that. He was so good that it was not unheard of for him to win both ends of a doubleheader with superb performances. On one occasion he allowed just five hits in back-to-back games on the same day. One reporter who described the twin bill, which occurred in 1942, called Seinsoth one of the finest pitchers in the entire Southern Association after he led his team to a pair of wins, 4-3 and 12-0. He allowed just a solitary hit in the first game and only four hits in the second game to bring his record to a sterling 23-8.

Despite his pitching and hitting prowess, Bill Sr.'s goal to play in the major leagues would have to be fulfilled by his son, Billy, who was born three years before his father's retirement from pro ball and six years before the St. Louis Browns, one of the worst franchises in baseball history, moved to Baltimore, Maryland, and drifted into history. His son displayed the same love for baseball that Bill Sr. did and perhaps even more skill, and it became clear to everyone early on that pitching and hitting would be the primary ambitions of Bill Seinsoth Jr. He was cut from the same cloth as his talented father, who after his playing days ended in 1950 worked as a truck dispatcher for twenty-five years before earning his real estate license in 1975. Young Bill had the ability, and starting in Little

League everyone could see that. All he needed were some breaks along the way to enhance his great skill. Unfortunately, good luck would never be his friend.

2

ARCADIA

"[As kids] we both wanted to be big-league players. It was nice [that we were] able to sign with the Dodgers because they were our hometown team. [Bill Seinsoth] was a prototype first baseman" **(Wagner 2015).**

–Tommy Hutton, former infielder for the Los Angeles Dodgers, Philadelphia Phillies, Toronto Blue Jays, and Montreal Expos

Like many homes in sprawling, post-war Arcadia, a quiet suburb nestled in the heart of Los Angeles County's San Gabriel Valley, the brick house at 935 South Tenth Avenue has changed considerably since 1947. Built the year after World War II ended and shortly before the birth of Bill Sr.'s son, the house appears small or cozy, as realtors might say. Bricks now cover the front from top to bottom, the trees are more resplendent, and gone is the thick ivy that blanketed many Southern California yards in the middle of the twentieth century; aside from the few shrubs, there is little landscaping. That's as it should be —Arcadia enjoys a moderately warm climate during most months, and regular droughts keep residents mindful of the need not to expend water on what some perceive as frivolities—plants. Hidden behind the spreading trees are two windows, one large and one small, that peek out upon an avenue where sidewalks run from block to block. Tenth Avenue in 1947 was probably not much different than Tenth Avenue today, just less substantial.

Bill Sr. embraces his wife, Jane, probably in the early 1940s
(*Seinsoth family photo*)

The Seinsoths—Bill Sr., his wife, Jane, their daughter, Janice, who at that time was just seven, and young Billy —moved into the home when the boy was twelve days old on April 16, 1947. A few years after that, when Bill Sr. played in Macon, Georgia, Jane and the kids followed the elder Seinsoth from city to city as his baseball career ebbed and time began to overcome him, but it was difficult for four people to keep up. Jane's main complaint was the schools that were available and the classes that were offered in other communities, namely those in the South—they were sometimes less advanced than those offered in the Arcadia Unified School District, she believed, and after a year she gave up and kept the kids in Arcadia. "When Janice started going to school we tried it for one year," she said. "The schools were so different— we went down South and some of the classes were more advanced, some weren't as advanced. She came home one day, crying, and said: 'They called me a damn Yankee.' It was just too hard to uproot her, as she had been going to school here in Arcadia" (Wagner 1991).

As a result, Janice was re-enrolled at Camino Grove Elementary School in Arcadia, where the other two Seinsoth children—Billy and Dauna—also attended when they were old enough. "After that, a couple times I would [travel to watch Bill Sr. play], but most of the time I stayed [home]," Jane said.

At that time, Billy was just beginning to walk. When he had that essential skill perfected and could scurry about without tumbling, it was not long before the throwing and catching that would become his trademark began to develop. His mother recalls the boy's foray onto a Macon minor-league baseball field, an environment he would not stray far from during all the years of his life.

"[Bill Sr.] was always throwing the ball to Billy, and he loved it," Mrs. Seinsoth said. "The first time he showed that he really had any interest in baseball was when my husband took him to the ballpark early and [Billy] went down into the dugout. The team did their warm-ups, then they went back in the dugout.

Best friends: Bill Jr. with sister Dauna in the early 1950s (*Seinsoth family photo*)

"Everyone started laughing and Bill looked out and young Bill was on the mound going through all the motions. He'd look over at first like he was going to throw to the first baseman, then he'd pretend to hit the ball and run the bases. He said that was the first time that he became interested in baseball" (Wagner 1991).

Bill Jr. had a vague recollection of his father's minor-league days. According to Seinsoth, his dad was playing for the Macon Peaches in 1950 when he was three years old, and at that point the elder Seinsoth began throwing to him. That's when it all began—and that's where everything ended, with baseball.

"I was never in Cub Scouts or anything like that," he told a reporter in 1969. "I just played baseball. That was everything until I went to USC. Since then I've developed other interests—my life is much more balanced now."

By kindergarten the dye had been cast. From then on baseball would remain in the young boy's blood, and later on in the young *man's* blood. In the same way that baseball had become a way of life for his father, one that enabled him to earn a fair living playing a child's game, it would soon become a way of life for young Billy Seinsoth.

Fortunately for the family, the opportunities available for kids to participate in organized athletics were numerous and wide-ranging in post-World War II Arcadia, and starting at a young age everyone wanted to play baseball. For children aged nine through twelve the Arcadia National, Santa Anita, and Arcadia Coast little leagues enabled boys to cultivate their interest in—and prowess at—the popular sport. The Arcadia Recreation Department afforded kids opportunities to remain sharp during the off season by participating in various slow- and fast-pitch softball leagues. Each of the three junior high schools offered baseball programs that allowed boys to compete against their friends from nearby schools while earning coveted athletic letters in the process. And local Pony, Colt, and Babe Ruth leagues gave players the expertise they needed to achieve a level of play that prepped them well for high school baseball. It was in high school where Bill Seinsoth first made his mark, a mark that remains as a beacon to aspiring, young baseball players from throughout the community. The symbol of that excellence still hangs on a wall inside the Arcadia High gymnasium, where the Seinsoth Award is seen by every student-athlete who enters.

The name "Arcadia" evolved from "Arcas," son of the Greek god Zeus—the god of thunder. Seinsoth's origin in a town named for the son of the god of thunder seems appropriate, as his home runs were thunderous. He was, it could be argued, another son of thunder, with Zeus-like features.

Arcadia was incorporated in 1903, thanks primarily to flamboyant Elias J. Baldwin, a nineteenth-century California pioneer who achieved his vast wealth through real estate speculation. Nicknamed "Lucky" due to his lucrative good fortune, Baldwin, a friend of lawman Wyatt Earp, might just as easily have been nicknamed "Unlucky" as a result of his four marriages and numerous suits alleging breach of promise or seduction (A Millionaire's Third Marriage 1884). He also was shot twice by angry women, escaping death both times—once when a bullet fired by the sister of a woman who was suing him for seduction nicked his head during a dramatic courtroom encounter (Historical Society of Southern California 2010).

In 1875 Baldwin purchased a swath of land where Arcadia is now situated for $200,000, roughly twenty-five dollars per acre (Historical Society of Southern California 2014). Led by Baldwin, who built residences on his sprawling property, homes were established, businesses were welcomed, and the community was invited to grow. Today, Arcadia is best known for two distinctions: the peafowl that still roam freely on city streets near Baldwin's former property, and high-profile Santa Anita Park, a thoroughbred track known for hosting the Breeders Cup world championship. Baldwin imported the peafowl following a trip to India, and the race track was founded on land that Baldwin transacted. Now testaments to his real estate prowess, the *Tarzan* movies of the 1930s and 1940s as well as other film and television productions, including a *Twilight Zone* episode, were shot in Arcadia on property Baldwin once owned, land that is now preserved within the confines of the Los Angeles County Arboretum and Botanic Garden.

It was in 1955, sometime after the Seinsoth family moved from Tenth Avenue roughly fifteen blocks west to Santa Anita Avenue, when eight-year-old Billy met John

Dawney while the two were students at nearby Santa Anita
School. Dawney was new to Arcadia, and the two, who
shared a birthday, became inseparable friends, enjoying
lunch breaks together in Mrs. Seinsoth's kitchen. "We
played every sport, we did everything together," Dawney
said. That included spending vacations together, with
Dawney joining the Seinsoths at a home owned by Billy's
maternal grandparents near Bass Lake, California, just
west of Yosemite National Park. (It was near there one
winter that his grandfather's body was found in his
smashed automobile at the bottom of a snowy cliff.) Young
Bill, in turn, joined the Dawneys at Newport Beach. They
also participated in a host of Arcadia Recreation
Department after-school and weekend activities, including
Saturday morning flag football games. The boys spent
summer afternoons at the Arcadia Plunge, a large pool
located at Arcadia Community Regional County Park. They
participated in various activities at the Youth Hut, a small,
converted home at First Avenue and Alice Street owned by
Arcadia Presbyterian Church, where both sets of parents
were at least somewhat active. They were involved in the
local chapter of Demolay, an organization dedicated to
preparing young men to become productive adults and
civic-minded leaders. And many mornings Dawney would
show up at his friend's house well before school, just as
Bill Sr. headed out the door for work. The boys would toss
a ball around as a fitting precursor to their day. At some
point Bill Sr. made a deal with the boys to install a
trampoline in the Seinsoths' backyard, something he
believed would help them strengthen their lower bodies for
baseball: if the boys would dig a pit to accommodate the
system, he would buy the trampoline. After excavating a
cavity large enough to drop an elephant into, the boys
spent long hours enjoying their new mode of exercise—
and, of course, strengthening their lower bodies for
baseball.

Billy began his baseball "career" across town from the
arboretum in the Arcadia National Little League, playing
for a team sponsored by the 7-Up Bottling Company,

Bill Jr.'s Little League team, the 7 Uppers, shows Seinsoth standing
next to his coach at top left, c. 1958

whom he would lead to an unheard-of 25-0 mark in 1958.
The league yearbook for 1959 notes that Seinsoth hit a
dramatic three-run home run the previous year as Arcadia
National's all-star squad beat the Santa Anita Little League
in the city all-star championship game, 3-2. A game earlier
Seinsoth had pitched a no-hitter to beat the Arcadia Coast
Little League. Teammates on 7-Up were Chris Arnold, who
would play alongside Seinsoth on Arcadia High's 1965 CIF
championship team and later for the San Francisco
Giants, and Dawney, who would become Seinsoth's high
school catcher and a teammate at USC.

His Little League successes aside, Seinsoth's parents,
to some extent, grew to regret their son's participation in
the program, even though he was a top player. "As an 11-
year-old he led the league in home runs," Dawney said
(Wagner 2015). Young Bill may have regretted those
years, too, although there is no record of the
disappointment or even anger he must have felt when
some in the league turned against him with a vengeance.
Why the fuss? Simple: Seinsoth dominated the Arcadia
National Little League, thanks primarily to a blazing
fastball that allowed him to handcuff the opposition while
hitting against opposing pitchers with ease. Within a
short while he was given the nickname "No-hit Seinsoth,"
and Billy became the most feared pitcher in the

Bill Jr. measures up to his father, Bill Sr. during the Little
League years, late 1950s (Seinsoth family photo)

community. His reputation only grew as the boy gained height, weight, and strength and progressed up through the baseball ranks, but not before rankled perpetrators initiated some dirty tricks designed to hasten his departure from the league. As his mother explained in 1991, the intimidation, which included telephone calls from parents, worked: "There were some problems, because they said he was too advanced—it was very traumatic for him. Our mailbox was blown up four times. The district attorney told me never to go to the mailbox without a long stick" (Wagner 1991).

Dawney supported Mrs. Seinsoth's recollection. "There was pressure [to get him out of the league] because he was so good," he said. "[People] felt that he shouldn't be playing with everybody else, and he was just dominating the league. As a pitcher, nobody could hit him. There was a lot of animosity involving the other coaches and parents" (Wagner 2015).

Arnold was a slick-fielding infielder for 7-Up when Seinsoth was a Little League teammate. In 1991, fifteen years after his subsequent professional baseball career ended, he recalled the controversy that swirled around the personable pitcher, who as a solid hitter and an overpowering left-handed hurler with great speed, was clearly in a league of his own.

"I remember one occasion when the opposing team just flat out asked him not to pitch," said Arnold, who played second base and third base for the San Francisco Giants. "They were terrified of batting against him" (Wagner 1991).

The parents of several players went so far as to demand the Seinsoths pull their boy out of the league, and they did just that. Because of the upheaval that the family and, in particular, young Billy experienced, Seinsoth eventually ended up leaving the league when he should have been enjoying his final year of play; as a result, his best friend Dawney led the league in home runs.

Clearly, the gratitude that Bill Sr. and his wife should have received as pillars of the Little League community was lost within the conflict. There would be no gratitude for Bill Seinsoth Sr. and his selfless work on behalf of the league, work that enabled the children of parents who may have opposed him to play Little League baseball. For him, there would mostly be regret.

In 1953 Bill Sr. helped to establish the Arcadia National Little League along with two other partners, raising funds to construct the present ball field and building the dugouts himself, and he must have been considered a youth baseball leader within the city of Arcadia. That a family so upstanding and dedicated to rearing children with lofty, yet realistic, goals for success should be threatened with physical harm because young Bill worked hard and excelled at the sport he loved must have seemed unconscionable to the Seinsoths, especially Bill Sr., who as a younger man also drove himself to excel at baseball. As a result of the fuss and fury they experienced, the Seinsoths decided to enroll their son in another youth baseball program, where he competed as one of the youngest players in the league. The 1960 Little League yearbook makes no mention of Seinsoth playing on the 1959 all-star squad, which would have been his final year and likely his most productive one, confirming his mother's recollection that she and her husband at some point grew tired of pushing back, especially at the expense of their son's peace of mind and possibly his well-being. In the long run, things worked out. While his peers remained content to play Little League baseball, the Seinsoths and Billy already had their sights set on something much larger: the big leagues.

The unfortunate scenario repeated itself when Seinsoth played in the local Babe Ruth League. He was so good that a groundswell of pressure again arose from those who felt he was too accomplished and should move on. It probably didn't help that as a fifteen-year-old playing in a preseason game Seinsoth had stepped on the foot of an opposing pitcher, a star player who was covering the bag in a close play at first base. The player was seriously injured and had to miss the entire season. "That set off a firestorm," Dawney said, adding that the misstep was an accident, but some believed the injury may have been caused intentionally and that Seinsoth was a dirty player. "It was just like Little League. He ended up going to another league and playing somewhere else" (Wagner 2015). His parents—Bill's dad was the team coach—once again pulled him out of the league and enrolled him in another program.

Young Bill during his junior high years, probably around 1960

Today, a scenario like the ones that so disturbed the Seinsoths during Billy's early years might be nipped in the bud by reasonable adults: the official Little League mission supports every athlete being given an opportunity to "[feel] like an important part of the team regardless of performance"—good or bad, presumably. It also supports players being given every opportunity to learn life lessons that have value extending "beyond the playing field," encouraging participants to "[learn] the skills, tactics and strategies of the game [so as to improve] as a player" (Little League Mission Statement 2015). The Babe Ruth League has similar tenets: "develop a strong, clean, healthy body, mind and soul; develop a strong urge for sportsman-like conduct; develop understanding of and respect for the rules; develop courage in defeat, tolerance and modesty in victory; develop control over emotions and speech; develop spirit of cooperation and team play; and develop into real, true citizens" (Babe Ruth League Sportsmanship Code 2015). As a young man with considerable talent, Bill Seinsoth met each of those standards. Despite his forced exodus from both Little

League and the Babe Ruth League, he would land on his feet, and bigger successes lay ahead. The real fun was about to begin.

3

HOMETOWN HERO

*"He was the best I ever coached. He was dominating,
intimidating. He was a man playing with boys"
(Wagner 1991).*

–Lani Exton, former baseball coach at Arcadia High School

Every community has a hometown hero, a thoroughbred
figure who was born and reared within the town's
borders, excelled at a high-profile sport, and instilled a
sense of deep community pride stemming from the
player's athletic successes. In the 1971 film *The Last
Picture Show*, Sonny Crawford was a local hero, a
homegrown player who led the charge on the football field
every Friday night for the high school team in a dying
West Texas town. Although the team's success is
marginal, and the young man has both his on- and off-
field failures, the townsfolk nonetheless take pride in the
football squad and each week glom onto the only player
they could remotely claim as a star: Crawford. Bill
Seinsoth was a local hero, only much more so. Not only
was Seinsoth a star in every sense of the word, but he led
his hometown Apaches to the only California
Interscholastic Federation baseball championship in the
high school's sixty-three-year history, equivalent to a
state title in regions of the country with fewer area codes.
So successful was Seinsoth, who also was a standout
high school basketball player, that local scribes latched

onto him at a young age, presenting his horsehide and hoops exploits to the reading public at every turn. As they say in the newspaper business, Seinsoth was good copy: strong as a bull, handsome as Adonis, heavy with talent, and loaded with personality and confidence. What's more, even as his successes mounted, and they did so almost rhythmically, Seinsoth never forgot where he came from, who helped him along the path to greatness and celebrity, and his unspoken responsibility to give something back to the community that had raised him and nurtured him athletically.

Although his death at an early age meant there weren't going to be many opportunities for the young man to repay the community that proudly claimed him as its own, one of his last efforts was the exhibition at Arcadia High School in the spring of 1969 just months before his accident. Seinsoth didn't have to be there that day, but he wanted to. It wasn't the first time he had levied his athletic success to assist his alma mater. In the years after he graduated, Seinsoth helped out on other occasions, counseling students who were having difficulty academically and athletically when administrators summoned him for assistance. Other occasions certainly would have arisen.

Unfortunately, Seinsoth ran out of time. The town's remembrance of the local boy who made good, etched into its collective memory through firsthand observation and the writings of its news scribes, would have to suffice.

Tony Torres, who played baseball in the Baltimore Orioles' organization after graduating from Arcadia High School, recalls his dad taking him to high school games in the early 1960s, where father and son watched intently as Seinsoth plied his pitching and hitting skills with cadence. The effort obviously paid dividends, and Torres, who also became a hard-throwing pitcher, hasn't forgotten the experience nor the trove of knowledge he gained from watching a true star in the making: "My dad took me to Arcadia High School games when I was in Little League, just to watch the strong left-hander. That was an accurate description of him: strong like a bull. He was left-handed all the way—threw left, batted left and just hit and hit and hit, as hard as I've ever seen."

Torres added, "He was incredible to watch. I remember standing there and watching in awe. He was just a great player in the Arcadia tradition" (Wagner 2015).

Later, the local newspaper introduced Torres to its readers as a possible heir apparent to the big left hander and the next great Arcadia pitcher in the Bill Seinsoth mold. Written in the paper in a 1966 column dubbed "Sportscope," an anonymous and well-read regular feature believed to have been penned by sportswriter DeMuth:

> **If there is one great prospect ahead for Lani Exton's horsehide squad it is Tony Torres . . . and it should be a great period if he follows former Little Leaguers like Bill Seinsoth . . . into the Campus Drive fold . . . (Sportscope 1966).**

With Bill Seinsoth, the comparisons flowed early. Torres didn't mind that a bit and said he still has that yellowed newspaper clipping, which half a century earlier his parents placed in a scrapbook. He remains flattered by the generous comparison given by the "Sportscope" author, which was surprisingly astute considering that Torres was only thirteen years old at the time: "It was quite an honor to be [talked about] in the same sentence with Bill Seinsoth," he said (Wagner 2015).

Other than Little League box scores and occasional references in related stories, one of the early public indicators of Bill Seinsoth's baseball capabilities against meaningful competition appeared in the local newspaper on March 24, 1963, when the youth was just fifteen and in his first year of high school. The baseball season, the first of three that Seinsoth would enjoy as a member of the varsity squad, was just getting underway, and already Arcadians were getting a taste of things to come. The headline that day read, "Apaches tripped 3-2; Bill Seinsoth fans 13" (Apaches tripped 3-2 1963). It may have been a coming-out headline for the teenager, who would prove more than capable of leading the baseball team for the next three years both as a hitter and as a fireballing, left-handed pitcher with, eventually, pinpoint control:

> **A cliff hanger was dropped by the Arcadia baseball team last Friday to Whittier High School, 3-2.**
> **Both pitchers went the distance, with Bill Seinsoth fanning 13 . . .**
> **In the fifth inning [Arcadia] got on the scoreboard for the first time. Seinsoth, with two away, doubled to center. Terry Mulleavy then singled to right, allowing Seinsoth to make the trip around (Apaches Tripped 3-2 1963).**

Oddly, after the second paragraph there was no mention of Seinsoth's overpowering presence on the mound, which resulted in all but a handful of the eighteen outs recorded by Arcadia that afternoon coming on strikeouts. Seinsoth also allowed only two hits during the game, something the writer also failed to note, in going the distance to record a complete game. Nonetheless, Bill Seinsoth was on his way.

Two weeks later Seinsoth fell to Earth during a home game at Arcadia High's Giambrone Field. Although picking up the win in a 5-4 victory over El Monte, he "blew up" in the third inning, as writer Stuart Roach described it, allowing three hits, two walks, and hitting two batters. He did strike out twelve, although he walked four, hit four batters—one player twice—and gave up six hits along the way. He singled once in three at bats, failing to score or drive in any runs (Roach 1963).

Seinsoth's seesaw performance didn't seem to discourage writer Roach, who remained optimistic in reporting on the game. "In the progress department, pitching has come right along," he wrote, noting that the

Photo sequence shows Seinsoth's great reach as a pitcher for Arcadia High School, c.1964 (*Arcadia High School photos*)

team's starting rotation of Seinsoth, Roger Boettger, and Warren Way "form one of the finest mound corps in the Pacific League" (Roach 1963).

The following month, in May 1963, Seinsoth turned things around, beating Montebello High, 4-3, to record another win. At that juncture Arcadia was a half game out of first place, and Seinsoth was getting stronger and gaining experience with each mound appearance.

"Arcadia hurler Bill Seinsoth tossed one of his finest games, striking out nine men on his way to the victory," it was reported. "He gave up only four hits and was brilliant, except for the sixth [inning]" when he gave up a single, hit a batter, then allowed a three-run home run (Seinsoth Sharp 1963). Seinsoth, who walked three, also went 1 for 2 and scored a run.

While his pitching performances had at times been dominant, Seinsoth was inconsistent, and wildness was an issue. Teammates had come to rely on his ability to strike batters out, but they also must have been wary of his tendency to walk and hit batters. The good and the bad seemed to be a tradeoff, but the team was winning ballgames, and that was what counted.

A season-ending story on June 9 put the 1963 season in perspective:

Under the guidance of coach Richard Carroll, a comparatively green crew of varsity horsehiders fought their way to a third-place finish in the always-tough Pacific League this spring.

The last game with El Monte was a mere formality. You couldn't convince Bill Seinsoth of this, though, as the soph connected for a bases loaded double in the final frame of that battle to give the Carrollmen an eleventh-hour 4-3 victory.

Seinsoth and Terry Malleavy, a standout all season, were rewarded for their playing skills at season end by being placed on the all-Pacific League first team (Carrollmen Capture Third Position 1963).

Between athletics, there were classes to attend and school assignments to complete, and Seinsoth did well in his studies. He eventually enrolled at an elite university, graduated from college in four years, and was tentatively planning to attend graduate school at USC, studying finance, after the Bakersfield Dodgers finished their season on September 3, 1969, although it's uncertain how he planned to complete his graduate studies with a baseball career in tow and the many and varied demands it placed upon his time. A comment Seinsoth made shortly before his death also indicated a commitment he apparently had to doing well in class: "I really wasn't too sad when [USC] didn't finish first in the Pacific-8 this year," he said in an interview with the *Bakersfield Californian* on August 23, 1969, two weeks before his death. "As it was, I hardly came out of my room during that time right before finals"—presumably because he was studying (Marin 1969). His sister, Dauna, vouched for him: "He was an A-plus, -plus, -plus [student]," she said. "He was an overachiever, he was exceptional" (Wagner 2015).

In 1963 and 1964, Seinsoth's sophomore and junior years in high school, the only extracurricular activities noted in the yearbooks were his participation on the varsity baseball and basketball teams. By his final year of high school, that had changed. His photograph appeared on six different pages in *The Arcadian*, the high school yearbook: his senior picture, a candid shot of him sitting in an architectural drawing class, a group photo of him alongside other members of the Lettermen's Club, and baseball and basketball photos, including a picture of him blocking a shot during a basketball game, a sequence of four photos with him pitching, and team shots in both sports. He was, without a doubt, one of the biggest men on the Arcadia High School campus.

His increasing popularity and an innate ability to excel at sports never went to his head, however. His stature as a high-profile athlete notwithstanding, Seinsoth made it a point to encourage his younger sister in her own extracurricular endeavors. An enthusiastic member of the high school's Chanteurs and A Cappella chorale groups, Dauna said her performances were sometimes attended by few people or none at all—with the possible exception of her faithful brother, who supported her wholeheartedly.

"Bill always had time for people," his sister said years later. "When I was singing in high school, we would have performances that often no one would attend. But I could always look out into the rows of empty seats and see Bill sitting there. He was that kind of guy" (Wagner 1991).

At least through high school Seinsoth attended Arcadia Presbyterian Church, which was situated just a few blocks from Arcadia High and the Arcadia Public Library, which was often the target of his long home runs. The church, a large congregation within walking distance of his home, which by that time was located on Santa Anita Avenue, was pastored by the Reverend James Hagelganz, who would one day marry close friend Dawney and his wife, Judy, and would figure prominently in the Seinsoth story. As he'd later write to a girlfriend, "I have gone to Arcadia Presbyterian Church ever since I can remember" (Seinsoth 1969). Seinsoth and his family are pictured in a church yearbook, and his parents—more so his mother, Dawney believes—were active participants in the congregation. "All through high school he went every

Sunday," Seinsoth's mother recalled. "If we didn't get there on Sunday, he walked" (Wagner 1991).

When his junior year began in September of 1963, the winds of change were about to blow hard across the landscape. Just two months later, on November 22, a lone assassin bearing a high-powered telescopic rifle and hiding in a Dallas, Texas, book depository would take the life of President John F. Kennedy, leaving the country, including the Arcadia High School student body, in stunned

Seinsoth appears dapper as a high school junior in yearbook photo, 1964 (*Arcadia High School photo*)

disbelief. With the country grieving, basketball season was by then in full swing, and the varsity schedule was probably released to the *Arcadia Tribune* on the day of the president's assassination—Friday, the day after the *Tribune*'s Thursday edition was published; it was posted in its entirety in the Sunday November 24 edition of the newspaper and served to remind readers that life would continue. The opening game of the 1963-64 varsity basketball season, against always tough Pasadena High, was scheduled for December 3, and for Seinsoth and his hopeful teammates, there was business to take care of if they had any hope of putting together a winning season.

From the get-go, business didn't proceed well for the squad, and things didn't get any better as the season progressed. Although Seinsoth finished as the team's second-highest scorer, the Apaches completed their season 3-18 overall and 2-10 in conference play, closing up shop near the bottom of the Pacific League hoops ledger. Perhaps because of the team's unsuccessful basketball campaign that season, the yearbook made only scant mention of either Seinsoth or his on-court ability to score and rebound:

> **Giving the varsity [coach] reason to be optimistic about next season is the fact that several juniors played key roles in the past season's play. Back next year will be Bill Seinsoth, 1964's second highest scorer; Doug Ball, a talented ball handler (and Seinsoth's close friend), Rich Ferguson; Buddy Ward; Chad Hughes; Rick Gable and Steve Brakebush (The Arcadian 1964).**

With a dismal basketball season now in the books, it was time for Seinsoth to regroup and once again train his sights on the number one sport in his life: baseball. The team's 1963 "building" season was by then a distant memory, and there was every possibility that the club would challenge for the CIF title in Division 4A, perhaps even bringing home a championship. Most observers, including new coach Lani Exton, believed Seinsoth's performance on the mound and at the plate would be key to achieving that goal. Exton, who replaced Carroll, died in 2013; however, in 1990 he put the talented left-hander's skills and abilities into perspective.

"He was the best I ever coached," said Exton, who also coached former major-league all-stars Steve Kemp of the Detroit Tigers, also an Arcadian, and Bochte of the Seattle Mariners. Arnold, a teammate of Seinsoth and the first Arcadian to make it to the major leagues, and a host of other big leaguers also trained under the respected coach. Exton added that Seinsoth's smiling intensity on the mound gave him an undeserved reputation for cockiness.

"He was dominating, intimidating," Exton said. "He was a man playing with boys. Bochte was a man playing with boys, but he was not as emotionally mature as Bill" (Wagner 1991).

At the outset of pre-league play it was anything but certain that 1964 could be the program's best year ever, as an early-season caveat was in place: Seinsoth, the team's highly touted pitcher, was finishing up his basketball season and had not turned out for a single baseball practice. One newspaper noted, "Yet to show up on the diamond are Bill Kay and Bill Seinsoth. Both boys should rate starting spots on the team as Seinsoth is listed as the top pitcher and also plays first base" (Apache Nine Opens Friday 1964).

As a result of his tardy arrival, the team started off shaky, and later in the season Coach Exton offered a logical explanation for the squad's early-spring woes: "Seinsoth had too much basketball and wasn't quite ready at the start of the baseball season" (Seinsoth Key for Arcadia 1964).

By early March, Seinsoth was at last on the baseball diamond and in fine pitching and hitting form. Not only did he combine to toss a three-hitter in leading the Apaches to their second straight win, an 8-0 shellacking of Temple City High in the fourth game of the season, but he also fanned four and collected two base hits in the contest. A week later, on March 10, he improved on the Temple City performance, combining to pitch a perfect game in a 9-0 win against San Marino High, collecting two more base hits. The baseball season, although still young, was shaping up nicely for the steadily improving Apaches and its young southpaw. In a newspaper story discussing the perfect game, headlined "Seinsoth, Leach Turn in for Perfect Game Over Titans," an unidentified writer waxed prosaic in proclaiming the gem by two of its premier pitchers:

> In Mercedes (as in Benz?), the SL stands for super light, but at Arcadia it stands for Seinsoth-Leach as the Apache hurling duo put together a perfect game against San Marino, 9-0, Tuesday (Seinsoth, Leach Turn in 1964).

In the following few games the baseball picture became even clearer: the varsity squad, led by Seinsoth, might just be the best in the history of Arcadia High, which had been established in 1952. The coveted California Interscholastic Federation playoffs, which would begin immediately following the culmination of Pacific League play, would be the team's ultimate test of its determination and ability.

By mid-March Seinsoth, despite his tardiness in joining the team, was hitting at a cool .451 clip and had struck out nineteen batters. The team, which had started the season 0-2, had since won four consecutive games and would win a fifth before finally losing, its record slipping to 5-3 after eight games. In that fifth win, on March 17, Seinsoth went 3 for 3 and scored three runs in leading his team to an 8-3 romp over cross-town rival Monrovia. On April 3 Seinsoth drove in all six runs, hitting a game-winning homer in the seventh and final inning, setting a school RBI record and leading his team to a narrow 6-5 win over Whittier. He went 3 for 4 in the contest, and his dinger, a 2-run shot, was blasted—where else?—in the direction of the Arcadia Public Library, a spacious domain where he clearly felt comfortable parking baseballs. Seinsoth also struck out eight batters in the game, which was too close for comfort.

By then Seinsoth was flying high; however, the season was still young. On April 27 a headline read "Seinsoth Pitches, Bats Apaches to 4-1 Decision" as the big lefty struck out nine batters and drove in three runs with a single that skipped under the right fielder's glove and rolled all the way to the fence. The Apaches, at last, were running circles around the competition—literally, in the case of Whittier High.

"No one could blame Whittier for believing the Arcadia baseball team was made up of just Bill Seinsoth Monday afternoon," it was reported. "For the second time this year the big southpaw went both ways [presumably hitting and pitching] to clip the Red Birds, 4-1" (Seinsoth Pitches, Bats Apaches 1964).

Despite the team's winning ways, the clouds that would chase Seinsoth throughout his life were beginning to form. Coach Exton once recalled that at some point during

Seinsoth's junior season a ground ball stuck him in the nose, fracturing it, although the incident apparently went unnoticed by the local news media. That summer, during separate beach outings, he would break it two more times when surfboards struck him in the face. In its August 30, 1964, edition the *Tribune* reported on one of those incidents that did not escape attention, although the story was not published until the following week:

> **Bill Seinsoth, the Sandy Koufax of CIF baseball last season, is sporting a badly bent face as the result of a surfing accident last week.**
>
> **Seinsoth's board was caught by a wave off Laguna Beach and struck him full in the face, causing a number of stitches to be required to repair the damage.**
>
> **However, no damage was caused to his prize left arm . . . (Bill Seinsoth Struck in the Face 1964).**

Dawney, who would captain the Arcadia High baseball team in 1965 and was Seinsoth's battery mate on the baseball diamond, was with his friend at Newport Beach, California, a popular Southern California beach hangout, on another occasion. According to Dawney, the two borrowed some surfboards and off they drove to try their luck in the waves. Unfortunately, their luck on that particular day wasn't especially good. Sometime during the beach outing a surfboard again popped Seinsoth hard in the face, breaking his nose. Dawney drove his friend to the emergency room at a hospital in nearby Costa Mesa, then telephoned Seinsoth's mother to report the accident. Mrs. Seinsoth knew that her son was able to take care of himself, and she elected not to drive down to the beach, opting instead to let the boys deal with her son's injury themselves. "He was a tough guy," Dawney said (Wagner 2015). To Dawney's knowledge, Seinsoth never surfed again.

As always, Seinsoth took the surfing accidents in stride. After the third break, doctors decided the nose should be rebuilt, and when a plastic surgeon asked Seinsoth to select the nose he preferred to receive from among a series of sketches he was presented, he chose a prominent one resembling his own. Explaining his lack of creativity in choosing the same nose that he was now discarding, Seinsoth said, "My friends wouldn't recognize me without this beak." Doctors complied and gave him the proboscis he requested. His sobriquet in high school? "The beak," Dawney said. "Bird bill," added Dauna [Seinsoth] Frazier (Wagner 2015).

Established in 1914, the California Interscholastic Federation is California's official governing body for high school athletics. One important disparity between California's athletic governing body, known as CIF, and those in other states is that California does not have a statewide champion in all sports. Instead, the CIF is divided into various regional sections and a champion for those sections is crowned. As a result, in many sports a CIF sectional championship is as coveted as a statewide championship in states that are smaller and do not have as distinctive a setup. In 1964, a CIF baseball championship was the closest to a state title that any team could get.

The Southern Section of CIF, encompassing Los Angeles County, has long been considered among the most competitive of the ten CIF regional sections. Well-known athletes who have participated in sports through the CIF include Walter Johnson (baseball), Louis Zamparini (track and field), Ted Williams (baseball), Jackie Robinson (baseball), Billy Casper (golf), Pat Haden (football), Tony Gwynn (baseball), Karch Kiraly (volleyball), Janet Evans (swimming), Tiger Woods (golf), and actor John Wayne (football). And, of course, Bill Seinsoth.

As the Pacific League campaign wound to a close, Arcadia finished in a three-way tie for first place at the end of conference play. At that point one thing was unmistakable: the team's road to a championship would be anything but easy. Looming large ahead of them was formidable Lynwood High, led by mound ace Greg Conger, who later played Triple-A ball in the Oakland Athletics organization before an arm injury forced him to retire with an ERA under 3.0 over seven minor-league seasons.

First in line with hopes of knocking off Arcadia in the CIF playoffs was Fontana High, and Seinsoth was at his gritty—although far from pretty—best. He pitched a complete game while striking out ten and walking two in a narrow 7-6 extra-inning win over the Steelers on May 15. Always dependable at the plate, he also collected a base hit and scored a run.

"Showing his workhorse ability more than ever was Bill Seinsoth, who chucked the full nine innings striking out 10 men," wrote one sportswriter (Roach 1964).

Next up was Serra, and again it was all Seinsoth from beginning to end. Starting his second consecutive playoff game, he survived seven errors and his own four walks to overcome a four-hitter by the opposition and pitch another complete game win, 3-2, on May 19. Seinsoth also knocked in a run in the first inning with a single— the only inning in which the Apaches would record a base hit.

By the quarterfinal game on May 22, just three days after his last complete game, the local newspapers were beginning to use words and phrases like "spectacular" and "one-man Apache nation" to describe the highly regarded Arcadia High School Apache, and for good reason. Thus far, he was 2-0 with two complete games under his belt and had put to rest any doubts that may have existed that he was a top-notch performer, especially under pressure. The question was, could he put together a third consecutive outstanding performance in a starting role? Coach Exton was banking on it.

With Anaheim aiming to pick up the spoils, Seinsoth was even tougher than he had been in the first two rounds, posting a four-hit, 4-0 win, and blasting a 400-

foot inside-the-park home run to drive in two runners. He also struck out eight during the seven-inning game, bringing his three-game playoff total to twenty-four. No wonder the left handed Arcadian was being compared with Dodgers ace Sandy Koufax and the entire Apache nation.

Round four, the semifinal game, pitted Arcadia against Mayfair on May 26, and the outcome was the same as in the previous three games. Working on four days' rest, Seinsoth threw another complete-game shutout, 3-0, although he was in trouble throughout the contest. Clearly tiring after endeavoring to complete his fourth complete game in eleven days, Seinsoth nonetheless struck out four and walked five in going the distance to record the win. He also went 1 for 2 to send the Apaches hurtling into the title game on May 29.

With one game standing between the underdog Apaches and a CIF title, first-year coach Exton again chose to go with Seinsoth as his starting pitcher. Facing Lynwood ace Conger, one of the premier pitchers in the country, Seinsoth would have his hands full, as would Conger in facing the seemingly indestructible Seinsoth. The game would mark Seinsoth's seventh consecutive start dating back to conference play and his fifth start in fifteen days, with all four of his previous performances ending in complete games—two of them shutouts. The tireless left hander with the arm of steel, himself one of the finest pitchers in the country, was ready to take on the toughest of all assignments: a championship game against the top-seeded team and a young man who had not lost a game the entire season.

Unfortunately for Arcadia, the title would elude them, at least in 1964. The game-weary Seinsoth was ineffective during the championship matchup against Conger, losing 7-1 to the formidable lefty while driving in Arcadia's only run with a single. While his pitching arm had finally let him down, he still managed to go 2 for 3 in the losing cause. Seinsoth's statistics for the five-game playoffs: 36 1/3 innings pitched over five complete games, four wins, and an earned run average of 0.96—all over an incredible span of just fifteen days.

"I really can't alibi, but I was pretty doggone tired," he said after the game (Jensen 1964).

Seinsoth also batted .428 and hit two home runs in taking the Apaches as far as they could go in the CIF playoffs.

"I had a very good day and our team had a very good day, and Bill was probably overworked," recalled Conger, one of only two pitchers to beat Seinsoth that season and a young man who vomited out of nervousness before every game—including the CIF finals.

> **It was quite a game. Clearly, we knew of Bill's reputation—I'm sure we had some of our coaches scouting him. My biggest concern, and it remained so throughout the game, was Bill's bat. I always thought that if he were to make it in the major leagues, and it's always an 'if' for anybody, he would make it as a position player—I didn't think he'd make it as a pitcher. He was a big, strong young man (Wagner 2015).**

Seinsoth's friend, Dawney, vividly recalls watching from the Arcadia dugout as Lynwood celebrated the championship with all the excitement befitting a CIF title. Every Apache watched, and as they did a sense of destiny began to build for 1965.

"We just looked at each other and said, 'We're going to do it next year for sure,'" Dawney said (Wagner 2015).

According to Conger, he and Seinsoth competed in a winter league later that year with a pitcher named Rick Dahlgren, who would face Arcadia in a critical game the following season. Conger and Dahlgren—son of Babe Dahlgren, who replaced Lou Gehrig to end the legendary Yankee first baseman's consecutive games streak—played on the same team, opposing Seinsoth. With residual animosity remaining between Seinsoth and Conger following the recently completed CIF finals, the two threw brush back pitches against their respective opponents,

Photo depicts ballplayers' view toward home plate, Seinsoth's domain, taken from a dugout at Arcadia High School, 2014 (*S.K. Wagner*)

which eventually incited fisticuffs involving some of the parents who were in the stands.

"Bill's dad came out of the stands and my dad came out of the stands and Babe Dahlgren came out of the stands," he said. "The police came and they stayed while we finished the game. Fortunately, Bill and I were smart enough to just duck under the fray. We had a discussion about who started the thing, but it never got to physicality" (Wagner 2015).

There was plenty of physicality among parents who left the bleachers, however. "There were bloody noses and broken ribs everywhere," Conger said. "It was a heck of a fight."

In more ways than one it had been a season of discontent for Seinsoth, although his statistics were nothing short of spectacular: he finished the spring campaign with an 11-2 record on the mound and a .405 batting average. Seinsoth and his cousin, Hutton, who played for South Pasadena High School, deservedly were named co-players of the year for the 1964 all-San Gabriel Valley high school baseball team.

"Nothing can be taken away from the terrific Apache southpaw," the *Tribune* wrote. "He held out much longer than anyone would have predicted, going at the terrific pace the playoff demanded (Roach 1964)."

The writer was correct. In one regard it truly was a terrific pace, at least for Seinsoth, and one that raised some eyebrows within the community, Seinsoth's mother said. After all, no other pitcher was given an opportunity to throw during the high-profile five-game playoffs. That had to leave some of the players—and their parents—grumbling. "There was quite a bit of flak at the time because coach Exton had him pitching every game," said Seinsoth's mother, whose husband—Bill Jr.'s father—would watch his son's games all by himself from a standing position beyond the centerfield fence, where his view of the entire field was unimpeded and he could unobtrusively leave whenever he wished. "He said that if he didn't think that Billy could do it, he wouldn't have him do it. Big Bill never interfered—he said that if he saw something that was hurting him he would interfere. He was very careful that [Billy] didn't throw too hard and that he didn't put his arm in jeopardy."

She added, "[Lani Exton] was a very fine coach, very conscientious" (Wagner 1991). Fortunately for her son, many of the innings he pitched in the playoffs probably involved quick strikeouts, which minimized the wear on his pitching arm and got his coach off the hook.

Finally, the long, drawn-out, and bittersweet 1964 baseball season had come to a close. With that, the team's hopes of someday winning a CIF title were only intensified, as the team's elite players—including Seinsoth, Dawney, and the future Giant, Arnold—would be returning in 1965. For them and the other juniors there would be one more chance to win a title before the core of the 1964 team graduated and went their separate ways. The difference was, Seinsoth had earned a reputation not only as a great pitcher and hitter, but for pitching long, hard, and often. Next season, the scouts would be watching him with both eyes.

4

PREP CHAMPIONS

*"We sat in the dugout after the [1964 CIF
championship] game watching [our opponents]
celebrate out on the field. We looked at each other
and said, 'We gotta [win] it next year for sure.' There
was no way we were going to lose. Bill Seinsoth was
the main reason we won in 1965."*

¬John Dawney, captain of the 1965 Arcadia High School
baseball team (Wagner 2015)

The summer of 1964 was a strange and difficult one
for Seinsoth, who was riding a cloud after leading his
team all the way to the CIF championship game. Not only
was he involved in serious surfing accidents on two
different occasions, but sometime after school ended
something much more ominous occurred, an incident
that might well have ended the young man's baseball
career—or his life—just as it was shifting into high gear.
While few details of the mysterious encounter were ever
revealed to either his family or friends, in a 1990
interview Seinsoth's mother did provide what little
information she was able to glean from her son, who
remained closed-mouthed about the incident forever
afterward.

According to Mrs. Seinsoth, her son was wrapping up
a getaway with friends at Balboa Island, a wealthy
Southern California bayside community, when an
unidentified assailant inexplicably assaulted him,

probably with a knife. As Seinsoth tried to defend himself, the man slashed him across his pitching hand, leaving a serious gash. Not wishing to upset his parents, who by then were hopeful that a future in professional baseball awaited him, Seinsoth insisted he had sustained the injury while changing a flat tire. However, the Seinsoths knew better, and they knew their son better than that as well. Little more was said about the incident, which Seinsoth kept quiet. When it came to talking about himself, he was unusually tight lipped.

Fortunately, the gash sustained on his left hand healed nicely, and by his senior year in high school Seinsoth and his reliable pitching arm were being followed by college coaches around the country. Those especially interested in securing his talents included Arizona State University, which offered him a scholarship to play baseball and basketball, the University of Texas, a fixture in the College World Series, and, of course, the USC Trojans, a perennial baseball powerhouse whose program was on the rise. No one wanted his services more than legendary head coach Rod Dedeaux, an ex-Dodger who went 1 for 4 in a brief major-league baseball career that spanned just two games with Brooklyn in 1935. By 1965 Dedeaux was a longtime family friend of the Seinsoths, and he knew well the youth's prodigious baseball capabilities, primarily through his own longstanding relationship with Bill Sr., whom he had met in the 1930s as their minor-league careers paralleled. Despite his keen interest in the youth, the younger Seinsoth's attention was focused on his senior year at Arcadia High. With school about to begin, there were more pressing matters for a high school boy to attend to—basketball and baseball among them—and Seinsoth managed to focus on sports in spite of any and all distractions that would come his way. There would be many.

The first distraction was basketball, and Seinsoth quickly underscored that he was more than a one-sport athlete. The aggressive Seinsoth led the basketball team in scoring with a 14.9 points per game average as Arcadia clawed its way to an 18-7 record and a second-place finish in the Pacific League. The team also earned a spot in the CIF tournament, although the Apaches lost to Centennial in the first round, 67-65.

"Paced by the high-scoring trio of Bill Seinsoth, Rick Gable and Rich Ferguson, Arcadia's varsity hoopsters fought to an 18-7 season record and second spot on the Pacific League totem pole," the 1965 high school yearbook reported. "With Ferguson pulling down rebounds, Gable pumping from the outside, and Seinsoth driving in for muscle

Seinsoth's flashes his characteristic smile in a varsity basketball yearbook photo, 1965 (*Arcadia High School photo*)

shots, Coach Vallie Robinson's crew compiled a 9-3 league mark, losing only to Monrovia twice and Whittier once" (The Arcadian 1965).

The Monrovia game on January 15 was a treat for fans, as it featured Fair Hooker playing for the Wildcats. Hooker, a local legend who scored twenty-one points and brought down twenty-three rebounds in the lopsided contest, went on to play six seasons with the National Football League's Cleveland Browns. Led by Hooker, Monrovia thrashed the Apaches, 67-34, with Seinsoth leading the Arcadia scoring attack.

"Bill Seinsoth and Gable gave the best Apache showings," read one press clipping. "Seinsoth showed the best shooting for the night, chalking up 13 points" (Wildcat Defense Buries Arcadia 1965).

With a subsequent loss to Centennial in the CIF playoffs Seinsoth's three-year prep basketball career was over, and it had been a sterling one. He was looking forward to better things, however, and his future unequivocally was in baseball. At Arcadia High, baseball practice under the guiding hand of second-year coach

Exton had already begun, and the team was committed to nothing less than winning the CIF title that had slipped through its grasp in 1964.

The Apaches had everything going for them in 1965, including a host of returning letterman—Bill Seinsoth among them—and a rebuilt Giambrone Field. Workers put the finishing touches on the field shortly before the baseball season began, enabling one of the most promising teams in the CIF Southern Section's Division 4A to open play with revamped base paths, rebuilt batter's boxes, new infield turf, and a carefully restored outfield. All systems were go.

Ready to go, too, was Seinsoth, who had played amateur ball in nearby Pasadena during the winter months and appeared to observers to have gained both height and muscle. It showed in his play, as local headlines attested: "Bill Seinsoth is Sharp in Four-Inning Effort," "Seinsoth Wild in Two-hitter," "Seinsoth Big Gun in Apache Win," "Seinsoth's One-hitter Numbs Cats," and "Seinsoth Hurls Second Shutout." When the dust had cleared, Arcadia had clinched its second consecutive Pacific League baseball title and was raring to challenge any and all comers in the CIF tournament.

"Bill Seinsoth is not only the premier pitcher for the Arcadia High School varsity nine, but he is easily the leading hitter," read a news account on April 8, 1965 (Seinsoth, Dold Top AHS Hitters 1965). At the time, the "leading hitter" was popping base hits at a .474 clip.

As the CIF playoffs began, the "premier pitcher," as the newspaper also described him, was more than prepared, wasting little time proving that Arcadia was the team to beat. In the opening round playoff game on May 21, Seinsoth pitched a five-hit shutout, striking out nine batters as Arcadia beat Excelsior, 4-0. Four days later, on May 25, Seinsoth again was the starting pitcher, throwing a three-hitter to knock off Loyola, 5-1. The game was played at USC's Bovard Field, which Seinsoth would come to know intimately over the following four years.

Seinsoth battery mate John Dawney displays his catcher's crouch for
Arcadia High School (*Courtesy of John Dawney*)

On May 28 Seinsoth hurled another complete game, striking out fifteen batters as Arcadia won again, beating Ventura, 3-1, in the CIF quarterfinals. Then, on June 1, Seinsoth pitched his team to a fourth consecutive playoff victory, a 2-1 squeaker over Lakewood in the CIF semifinals.

On June 4, in the CIF finals against Warren, Seinsoth was magnificent, working on three days of rest to toss a three-hit shutout while striking out five in a 5-0 victory that gave Arcadia its first and only baseball championship. In the five playoff games over fifteen days, Seinsoth had started, completed, and won each contest, including three complete games over the final eight days. The big southpaw hurled two shutouts, struck out thirty-six batters, and over the final three games faced ninety-four hitters without walking a single player. His numbers on the season were a masterful 15-1 record and an ERA of 0.72. He also struck out 145 batters in 116 1/3 innings and batted an impressive .390. The losing pitcher that day? Rick Dahlgren, son of Babe Dahlgren and a player who observed the melee instigated by Seinsoth and Conger earlier in the school year.

"While our entire team was great, Bill Seinsoth was the main reason we won in 1965," team captain Dawney said. "He pitched five complete game playoff wins in fifteen days, including three in eight days and two shutouts—one of them in the championship game. It was clear he had a bright future" (Wagner 2015).

The trove of scouts that had followed Seinsoth through the playoffs were not disappointed, and over the ensuing weeks events transpired quickly. He was named CIF player of the year after the championship game, and his family wasted little time announcing that Bill Jr. would attend USC on a baseball scholarship, which eventually morphed into an academic scholarship, turning down an offer from Arizona State at the eleventh hour (DeMuth 1967). In making the announcement, the elder Seinsoth also said that his son would remain at the university for a minimum of two years, a pledge the young man more

Left photo: Catcher John Dawney, flanked by Seinsoth (right) and Coach Lani Exton, poses for photo with the team's California Interscholastic Federation championship trophy. Right photo: an elated Arcadia High coach Lani Exton gives a smiling nod to his equally happy star pitcher, Bill Seinsoth, c. 1965

than lived up to despite entreaties from the different major-league teams that would draft him in each succeeding year—four in all, with the Dodgers drafting him twice.

Capping off a whirlwind week, on June 8 the Houston Astros selected Seinsoth in the fifteenth round of the June regular phase of the amateur entry draft, the first ever major-league draft of high school and college-age players. The draft soon became a mainstay for major-league teams interested in selecting promising young ballplayers, and Bill Seinsoth was certainly one of those.

Also drafted was teammate Arnold, who surprisingly was chosen before Seinsoth—in the eleventh round. Arnold, who would become the first player in the school's history to play in the major leagues, credited Seinsoth with facilitating that honor in an interview many years later: "Because Bill was so good, the scouts began coming to our games," he said. "Someone noticed me and the end result was a career with the Giants. I was the first player from Arcadia High to sign a professional contract, and it was largely due to Bill Seinsoth."

Arnold added, "Even in those days he was the consummate professional. When it got down to baseball he was all business" (Wagner 1991).

As Seinsoth prepared to enroll at USC, the California Interscholastic Federation paid the all-American boy a high compliment: on September 1, 1965, the CIF released its media and record book with the Arcadian's smiling face on the back cover. He had become, it seemed, the organization's pinup boy for athletic success and one of its proudest protégés over the course of the 1965 school year, someone whom organizers were pleased to brag about in conspicuous fashion as he left the confines of Arcadia High and Giambrone Field.

"You don't have people like Bill come through the student body every day," reflected Richard W. Cordano, who was principal at Arcadia High when Seinsoth was a student, shortly before his own death. "He was a very unique person" (Wagner 2015).

Although he didn't know it at the time, Seinsoth would rely on that uniqueness, perhaps subconsciously, to earn even greater successes while a student-athlete at USC. As he prepared to enter a new and exciting phase, life, once again, was Bill Seinsoth's oyster.

5

USC CALLING CARD

"[My dad] had his eye on Bill, Jr., before he even started high school. When he came in he was a superstar."

–Justin Dedeaux, former assistant baseball coach at USC

Like John Wooden in basketball and Bear Bryant in football, Rod Dedeaux's name is synonymous with the sport he coached for nearly half a century: baseball. Dedeaux won more NCAA championships than either Wooden (with ten) or Bryant (six), and his five consecutive baseball titles between 1970 and 1974 is a mark that may never be broken. By comparison, no other baseball coach has ever won more than two championships in a row.

Born Raoul Martial Dedeaux on February 17, 1914, in New Orleans, Louisiana, Dedeaux attended Hollywood High School in Southern California, where he was an all-city shortstop in 1930 and 1931. He then excelled as a shortstop at USC, where he played from 1933 to 1935 and was team captain his senior year—just as Seinsoth was. Highly regarded for his talent on the field, Dedeaux was signed as an amateur free agent by Casey Stengel's Brooklyn Dodgers after his college career ended in 1935, although his tenure with the organization ended almost as abruptly as it began.

Dedeaux was assigned to play for the Dodgers' Dayton, Ohio, affiliate, where he hit .360 and earned a promotion to the big-league Dodgers roster toward the end of the 1935 season. He made his major-league debut on September 28, 1935, and the final game of his major-league "career" was—the following day. During those two games he went 1 for 4 with an RBI. A broken vertebrae suffered while swinging a bat the following year effectively ended his major-league career just as it was beginning, and Dedeaux finished with a "lifetime" batting average of .250. He bounced around the minor leagues for several seasons but was unable to work his way back up to the big club, eventually retiring to pursue other interests. One of those interests was his alma mater—USC.

Fortunately for the world of college athletics, Dedeaux reinvented himself seven years after his major-league debut and returned to the college baseball scene in 1942 as the youngest collegiate head coach in the history of the sport: he was only twenty-eight at the time. Just six years later, Dedeaux, co-coaching with Sam Barry, won his first national championship at USC. There would be others, often in short succession. In addition to the 1948 title, Dedeaux won championships in his own right in 1958, 1961, 1963, 1968, 1970-1974, and 1978. His 1,342 wins over forty-five seasons are the fifteenth most among all college coaches, and many of those who achieved more victories did so at less prominent schools such as Lubbock Christian University, High Point University, Marietta College, and Cumberland University. To achieve so many wins for a high-profile Division I university, resulting in eleven national titles, is truly a remarkable accomplishment.

After coaching nearly 200 professional ballplayers and sixty major leaguers, including Tom Seaver, Fred Lynn, Dave Kingman, Randy Johnson, Steve Kemp, and Mark McGwire, Dedeaux retired after the 1986 season with eleven national championships and twenty-eight conference titles to his credit. When he retired he had more victories than any other college baseball coach in history and a .699 winning percentage. His salary at the end of his USC career? A mere one dollar per year.

On the USC campus in downtown Los Angeles, situated near Heritage Hall and the USC Athletics Museum, rests a solitary, time-worn plaque. It reads, modestly: *Bovard Field. This plaque marks the perimeter of Bovard Field, which for many years was the practice and playing field for Trojan athletics. This site is dedicated to the athletes who contributed to the scholastic and athletic achievements of the university.*

Bill Seinsoth was one of the athletes who graced Bovard Field. As he prepared to leave the family home to attend a university that boasted a rich history of baseball excellence, Seinsoth was well aware of the USC athletic legacy he was stepping into. He was leaving home for an uncertain future, one that he knew would involve baseball. That was the only certainty. Where would he live and who would be his roommates? What academic course would he study? Would he make the grade, either as a student or as an athlete—or both? In juggling the rigors of baseball and academics, would he graduate on time or at all, perhaps choosing instead to leave his studies behind and sign a major-league contract? And what about the many high school friends he was saying good-bye to, friends like Dawney, his battery mate at Arcadia High, as well as prep basketball teammate Doug Ball, and Bill Caldwell—would they stay in touch as their lives spun off peripatetically? While there were numerous questions and few answers, there was one certainty: baseball. The sport he loved to play and was inordinately good at would continue to be a big part of his life for at least the next two years, hopefully much longer. During that time, Bovard Field on the campus of USC, named for George F. Bovard, the school's fourth president and its second-longest serving chief executive, would be his baseball home away from the dormitory, fraternity, or apartment—wherever he happened to live in any particular year while at USC.

If Bovard Field was his home, then Dedeaux would be his surrogate father, at least while Seinsoth was absent from Arcadia. What better proxy for the youth, his family must have thought? Dedeaux's friendship with his father, Bill Sr., went way back to the Great Depression, when both played baseball—Bill Sr. in the minor leagues and briefly with the St. Louis Browns, and Dedeaux briefly with the Dodgers. Four years apart in age, they met when the elder Seinsoth, the younger of the two, was in high school. As a result, Dedeaux knew Bill Jr. when he was just a lad, and the ex-big leaguer began to take notice in earnest during the boy's Little League years, when Seinsoth was growing in leaps, gaining heft, hitting with power, and demonstrating pitching speed way beyond his ten years. Dedeaux was a consummate old-school baseball man, and he knew talent when he saw it. It didn't matter what age that talent was, and Seinsoth, although young, was certainly a prospect in the eyes of a man committed to winning baseball games and bringing home national titles. Although the boy was only a pre-teen, Dedeaux had hopes for his future, hopes that would involve bringing him to USC to help the university win those titles. Eight more years, and young Bill might be ready to join the USC family. Dedeaux could wait, and the time would pass quickly, he believed.

The time did fly by, and at last the defining moment of Bill Seinsoth's life up until that point had arrived. As he slammed shut the door of his Arcadia home, Seinsoth had no idea the great excitement and range of unforeseen difficulties the next four years, his *final* four years, held in store for him. That wasn't important. Seinsoth greeted every challenge with vigor and enthusiasm, and he usually came out a winner, although oftentimes worse for wear.

Once on campus, Seinsoth took up residence in Marx Tower along with other Trojan baseball players, later joining a fraternity that made national headlines in 1959 when a pledge choked to death on a piece of raw liver during a hazing ritual: Kappa Sigma. Justin Dedeaux, architect of the teams that helped his father win five consecutive national titles, said freshmen were encouraged to refrain from joining fraternities until after their first year.

"We'd always tell them not to join a fraternity right away," Dedeaux said. "We were particularly concerned their freshman year because we wanted them to make grades. I'd always tell them to wait until they were a sophomore to join a house" (Wagner 2015).

Seinsoth, a finance major, apparently heeded that advice, which likely came from Dedeaux's father rather than himself, and friends said he did not pledge the fraternity until early in his sophomore year, residing in the dorms until moving into the Kappa Sig house as a junior; during his senior year he lived off campus with friends. The fraternity's description in *El Rodeo*, the USC yearbook, may lend a hint as to why the young man, who probably was in demand by several fraternities, chose to join that particular Greek house, described by teammate, fraternity brother, and college best friend Buzz Shafer as a jock house: "Kappa Sigma Fraternity is dedicated to full participation in inter-fraternity and university affairs. Its members, conscious of the opportunities offered by the university for fuller development, have entered every phase of campus activities. Sports, service groups and campus offices have come to the brotherhood in the past year" (El Rodeo 1966). Listed as the fraternity's "most prominent members" were Bill Cunerty, sports editor for the *USC Daily Trojan*, Mike Hull, a varsity football player, and Olympic swimmer Gilchrist, captain of the USC swim team (El Rodeo 1966). Gilchrist had competed in the 1964 Olympic Games in Tokyo and would swim again in the 1968 Mexico City Games. Bill Seinsoth was hoping for the same kind of success in his own athletic specialty.

Fraternity brother Tom Shenk and others remember Seinsoth as popular with the ladies, and during his college years he had at least two steady girlfriends. However, the fraternity and his social life aside, it was baseball that Seinsoth really pursued with a passion.

USC's 1966 freshman team: Seinsoth is seated front row, fourth from left; Coach Jerry Merz is next to him on his left. Future longtime major leaguer Tom House, a close friend of Seinsoth, is seated next to the team trainer. (*USC Athletics*)

That was the primary reason why he chose to attend USC in the first place, that was the reason why USC elected to offer him a scholarship, and there was no mistaking the young man's top priority: to succeed at baseball, using the time spent at USC to both help the baseball program and advance his goal of becoming a major-league baseball player. Arcadia High was his first such springboard, one that landed him at USC. USC became his second springboard, eventually catapulting him to the Dodgers organization. The Bakersfield Dodgers were to be his third and final springboard, presumably vaulting him to the Los Angeles Dodgers at some point in the early 1970s.

If Seinsoth had high hopes for his years at USC, it was axiomatic that the university, in particular the baseball team, had high hopes for the years that Seinsoth would be at the school. Those hopes would soon be nurtured on the freshman squad, where the pitcher/first baseman became a team leader.

"In those days freshmen had to play on the freshman team," Justin Dedeaux said. "Bill was extremely confident, he had no doubt about his abilities. He knew

Seinsoth clowns with USC teammate and close friend Buzz Shafer, 1966 (*Courtesy of Buzz Shafer*)

he had the gift, but it took him a little while to adjust. When he came in he was a superstar. [We thought], 'This is a savior.' I think that was hard on him and there was a lot of pressure [to succeed]" (Wagner 2015).

The local newspapers may have added to that pressure, as they continued to follow him after he left high school and all during his freshman year in college. The media loved him and, through their always-positive coverage, seemed to wish him the best.

"Bound for the University of Southern California in the fall, the youngster has not only been playing ball all summer, but every morning at 8:00 he is on the job at the Douglas Aircraft plant at Long Beach, which means a long day for the all-CIF player of the 1965 baseball season," the hometown *Tribune* wrote on August 8, 1965. "His team plays two and three games a week and practices after he finishes his day's work at Douglas" (Seinsoth Hits College 1965).

The first mention of Seinsoth's name in the USC student newspaper was in late September 1965 shortly after he arrived on campus. In noting that USC coach Dedeaux had snatched away the Philadelphia Phillies' number-one draft pick, future big leaguer Mike Adamson, the *Daily Trojan* also announced that Seinsoth would be joining Adamson on the freshman pitching staff; the two would be roommates during their freshman year.

"Coach [Dedeaux] put us together in the dormitory, Marx Tower—we were on the third floor," confirmed Adamson, who later played three seasons with the Baltimore Orioles before an arm injury forced his retirement. "If I remember correctly, Bill and I were the only two [players] on full [scholarships] as freshmen. We were different, but we got along well. I remember going out to Bill's house several times our freshman year to do laundry. He was a good guy."

According to Adamson, Seinsoth was well organized, much like he played on the baseball diamond. "He was meticulous. His side of the room looked a whole lot better than my side. Just like with baseball, he took everything seriously and did everything in the correct steps" (Wagner 2015).

Others on the frosh team that season were future Atlanta Braves pitcher Tom House, Jay Jaffe, Rich Schaffer, and Buzz Shafer. It was Shafer's family that would play a key role in Seinsoth's final days.

"The players were a close-knit group—many played together through the 1968 championship," said Jerry Merz, the freshman team's head coach in 1966 (Wagner 2015). In leading his team to a first-place finish in the newly established Freshman Baseball Conference of Southern California, Merz did double duties as a Triple-A player in the San Francisco Giants organization that season.

Seinsoth began his freshman season strong, and there was every indication he would live up to all of the expectations that had been heaped upon him since his graduation from high school. He hit the ball hard, connected often, was going for distance, and he pitched with the same level of confidence and ferocity that he had demonstrated in high school. Unfortunately, despite the team's 6-2 start, probably few people outside of the USC baseball program cared, as the school newspaper candidly reported:

> **No one pays attention to freshman baseball teams, naturally, but this one might bear watching. It features the CIF player of the year Bill Seinsoth, who is currently leading the team in batting with a .458 mark and 12 runs batted in [after eight games] (Freshman Baseballers Win 1966).**

As a result of his play, the local papers loved it whenever Seinsoth traveled to nearby ballparks for games. It gave them another opportunity to write "local boy makes good" stories. On March 3, 1966, the day after that *Daily Trojan*

Jerry Merz, Seinsoth's coach his freshman year at USC

article appeared, Seinsoth went 2 for 4 with a single and a double in an 8-2 loss to Pasadena City College (PCC), his best friend Dawney's team, at Bovard Field. On March 11 the *Pasadena Independent* took notice following another loss to PCC. "Bill Seinsoth, all-CIF-er at Arcadia High, was a visitor at PCC's Thurman Field Wednesday with the SC freshmen. The big first baseman had a hit and a run batted in as his team dropped a 6-5 squeaker to the Lancer nine" (Pickard 1966).

By May 15, with his freshman season completed and a 13-3 record in the books, a *Tribune* headline conferred upon Seinsoth the title "No. 1 star of Trobabes," the media's nickname for the Trojan freshmen team:

> **Bill Seinsoth picked up at USC where he left off at Arcadia High School, leading the Trojan freshman**

baseball team in hitting and pitching in the season just completed.

The 1965 CIF [4A] Player of the Year gave up just two earned runs in 21 innings for an ERA of 0.86 and batted .375 to lead the Trobabes in both departments. He drove in 30 runs to tie for the club lead and cracked five home runs, second on the team.

Seinsoth played first base most of the year, gathering 36 hits in 96 at bats. He struck out 19 enemy batsmen and finished with a 1-1 won-lost record.

The Trojan frosh posted a season record of 19-9-2, and finished first in the new Freshman Baseball Conference of Southern California with 13-3 (No. 1 Star 1966).

The freshman season had been tip-top for the team as a whole, exposing a number of potential varsity stars. For Seinsoth, it had been all that he and the varsity coaches who had encouraged him to attend USC had expected. With his rookie statistics prorated out to a 162-game major-league season he might have recorded 200 to 240 hits, 25 to 30 home runs and 150 to 180 RBI. His pitching stats and batting average were equally brilliant, speaking volumes for themselves, and despite the higher level of competition, Seinsoth's batting average dropped only fifteen percentage points from his magnificent senior year at Arcadia High.

In 1991, Jaffe, Seinsoth's freshman teammate in 1966, who as USC's center fielder in 1968 played a big role in its quest for a national championship, described Seinsoth as "bigger than life," adding, "There's no question he would have had a great major-league career" (Wagner 1991).

In 2014, nearly twenty-five years later, Jaffe's recollection—and opinion—of his friend and teammate had not diminished a bit.

"He was bigger than life," Jaffe said. "Bill was such a strong guy, with even a stronger personality. He was a born winner and he hated to lose. Fortunately, we seldom lost" (Wagner 2015).

In June of 1966 the Houston Astros' claim on Seinsoth, one that effectively began when the club drafted him in the fifteenth round of the 1965 high school and college baseball draft, expired despite the club offering him a reported $24,000 to sign (Sportscope: Blood Stays 1966). The expiration assured that Seinsoth, who by then had become a legitimate major-league prospect, would remain at USC through his sophomore year in college. The *Tribune's* Old Scout wrote in his Sportscope column:

> **Rod Dedeaux will get the Seinsoth bat on the varsity next year and then maybe some big-league team will come up with enough coin and fringe benefits to lure the Seinsoth name onto a contract. He should be worth at least 200 grand by today's standards of bonus, for he figures to be just as lethal with the ash in the spring of 1967 as he has been for the past four springs (Sportscope: The Old Scout 1966).**

Two weeks later, as if to punctuate the end of Seinsoth's brilliant freshman season, the Old Scout was back at it, waxing optimistic that Arcadia's favorite son would someday be playing in big-league flannels.

> **Everybody is satisfied that Seinsoth's bat would make him a major leaguer someday. Of course, he plays first base with a lot of poise. That's the spot his dad has played for years, and for a kid a year out of high school he handles the initial cushion [i.e., first base] defense like a veteran (Sportscope 1966: The Old Scout).**

As his freshman year of college came to a close, there was widespread optimism that 1967 would be Bill Seinsoth's coming-out season. Rod and Justin Dedeaux, both of them pros at evaluating baseball talent, knew full well how to build upon numbers such as Seinsoth's. While the Trobabes were putting together a winning season, the varsity would lose in the semifinals of the College World Series to eventual champion Ohio State by the narrowest of margins—1-0. As the next varsity season, Seinsoth's first as a Trojan, loomed formidably on the horizon, the highly regarded father/son combination of Rod Dedeaux and his son, Justin, had to be smiling at what lay ahead.

6

SAVIOR IN CARDINAL AND GOLD

"I always thought Bill would have been a great major leaguer. The rap on him was that he couldn't run well. You don't have to run well when you're running around the bases [after] hitting the ball out of the ballpark."

¬Jay Jaffe, former outfielder at USC

As a star player at an athletic powerhouse, Bill Seinsoth was first and foremost a perfectionist. While other aspects of his persona may not have been perfect, most observers, including former teammates and coaches, agree that Seinsoth was perfection in motion, at least when it came to baseball. He could hit for average and power. He could pitch with speed. He could play first base as deftly as anyone. And he moved with celerity, able to quickly shift right or left in order to traverse all of the territory that a solid first-baseman must cover.

The only thing Seinsoth couldn't do perfectly was run, however, given more time he probably would have figured out a way to do that, too. It was against his nature to do anything less than perfectly, a quality he probably acquired from his multi-talented father, who himself played first base when he wasn't on the mound.

"To me, there's no such word as 'can't'—I expect perfection in myself," Bill Jr. once said, borrowing an imploration from USC coach Rod Dedeaux, himself a perfectionist who walked the walk (Arnold 1967). According to his son, Justin, to motivate his players Dedeaux would tell them, "My tastes are simple: all I demand is perfection" (Wagner 2015).

Seinsoth sought excellence with a vengeance, something former pitcher Jim Barr, a teammate at USC and former major leaguer, recalled. "Anyone who remembers Bill knows how hard and intensely he worked," Barr said. "Bill always wanted his practicing to be as perfect as possible so that he could be as good as he wanted in the game. I [can] still see him taking batting practice and putting the mental intensity into each swing.

"When he was throwing, same way—each pitch had to be where he wanted it. I would like to think that I learned a lot about practicing just by watching Bill. That is why he would have been a very good pro, always working at it, always improving" (Wagner 2015).

If improvement didn't come quickly, Seinsoth was probably disappointed. That was evident in letters to a girlfriend, Gaye Gammon, now Gaye Farr, toward the end of his life when he felt he wasn't performing up to his own high standards as a member of the Bakersfield Dodgers. However, even on rare occasions when he worried that he was failing to make the grade, Seinsoth never backed off from the game he loved. It was always baseball, baseball, baseball.

"There's nothing I'd rather do than play baseball," he wrote Gammon in 1969. "I feel lost, anxious when I'm not playing it" (Wagner 1991).

Fraternity life suited Seinsoth, and he remained active with Kappa Sigma throughout college. At six foot two and between 210 and 220 pounds, he was a formidable tight end on the fraternity's championship intramural football team, and because of his size he evolved into an undeclared protector of sorts when fraternity members needed security. Once, when a rival fraternity doused the

Kappa Sig house with an assortment of rotten vegetables, Seinsoth joined his friends in an attempt to drive the perpetrators away. However, on that occasion he met his match in the person of a rare athlete who was bigger and stronger than he was: Bob Klein, a tight end on the 1967 national championship football team. Klein, who later played for the Los Angeles Rams, was 6'5" and 235 pounds, and he put Seinsoth in a bear hug and slammed him to the ground according to Shenk, who once roomed with Seinsoth. Even Goliath met his match, although Klein was obviously a much larger version of David.

　　To remain sharp, work on any baseball shortcomings he perceived, and generally stay involved in the game during the summer, Seinsoth shifted his focus to the subarctic terrain of Fairbanks and the Alaska Goldpanners, an elite baseball club established in 1960 as an independent barnstorming squad and whose roster of famous alumnae reads like a *Who's Who* of major-league baseball. Since the team was established, its membership has included such notable ballplayers as Hall-of-Famer Tom Seaver, all-time home run leader Barry Bonds, six-time major-league all-star Graig Nettles, four-time all-star Andy Messersmith, two-time all-star Rick Monday, two-time home run leader Dave Kingman, former big-league all-star Steve Kemp, six-time Gold Glove winner Bob Boone, and many others. With teammates like Boone, future big leaguer Jim Nettles, and USC colleagues Sheldon Andrens, Rich Schaffer, Mike Adamson, and Tom House on the 1966 Goldpanner squad, the latter two eventually playing in the major leagues, Seinsoth's first season in Fairbanks went exceedingly well.

　　Under manager H. A. "Red" Boucher, the Goldpanners went 50-13 that summer, with the newly itinerant Seinsoth at first base hitting a more than respectable .315. Although others in the lineup hit for higher average than

Seinsoth keeps a sharp eye on the ball while playing with the Alaska Goldpanners, an elite summer college baseball team, c. 1967 (*Nelson's Professional Photography*)

big number eighty-eight, including team MVP Boone at . 382, Seinsoth was just getting warmed up. The following summer at Fairbanks would be his big-number season with the top-flight group of college athletes, and over the course of his three seasons as a Goldpanner, Seinsoth would leave an ineradicable impression, making the list of all-time top Goldpanner performers in numerous offensive and other categories. Those included most games played in a career (sixth), most consecutive games played (second), most career at bats (fourth), most career runs scored (fourth), most career hits (fourth), most doubles in a season (ninth), most home runs in a career (tenth), and most RBI in a career (third). His position in the top ten for each of those categories has held up for nearly fifty years.

During their Goldpanner seasons, Seinsoth and Boone enjoyed a good relationship, and they socialized on occasion. It was Boone, a third baseman, who in one odd sense may have made Seinsoth a better first baseman, at least while they played in Alaska. In Fairbanks, the sun hung menacingly over third base for much of the game. To spare his friend the challenge of having to look directly into the glare when receiving his throws from third, Boone would fire the ball over to Seinsoth on one bounce.

Sheldon Andrens, who as a Goldpanner teammate once roomed with Seinsoth before continuing on to play Double-A ball with the Cincinnati Reds organization, recalls him as a fierce competitor who was committed to protecting his teammates above everything else—another quality he likely inherited from his father, whose quick temper was known to get him into trouble with opposing teams.

"One day, I arrived at the clubhouse to find all of my bats broken," said Andrens, noting that the name of an opposing player had been scrawled on each bat. Bill told me, 'Don't worry, we'll take care of it'" (Wagner 2015).

Later in the game the offending player ended up on first base, held on by Seinsoth. Andrens recalled that Goldpanner pitcher House threw over to Seinsoth five times in an effort to pick him off, and each time Seinsoth smacked the runner extra hard in the chest with his glove and ball. On the sixth throw Seinsoth swatted him across the knee, hyper extending it and leaving him writhing in pain on the ground. Angered by the attack on his player, third base coach Sam Suplizio started off across the infield toward Seinsoth, intent on paying him back for the perceived indiscretion. A teammate of Suplizio grabbed him and held him back.

"What are you *doing*?" asked Suplizio, who may have been overconfident about his retaliatory capabilities.

"Saving YOUR LIFE," the teammate said, implying that Seinsoth, at six foot two and 220 pounds, would likely dismantle Suplizio, who was five foot eleven and 175 pounds (Wagner 2015). You didn't mess with Bill Seinsoth, something every player on his team grew to appreciate. That level of respect is the mark of a professional, a distinction Seinsoth was constantly striving to achieve.

"Everyone looked up to him," Andrens said. "He was the kind of player who made you play better because you wanted him to think you were good" (Wagner 2015).

Not coincidentally, House and Seinsoth developed a reputation for picking off runners. "I would [throw over to first] and he would drop that big old right knee of his and [block the] bag," House said. "He had great game sense. He could play the game" (Wagner 2015).

The following summer Seinsoth played the game exceptionally well. In fifty-five games as a sophomore Goldpanner he hit .382 with seventy-three hits, twelve home runs, fifty RBI, and fifty runs scored; he even recorded three stolen bases despite his lack of speed on the base paths. Over the span of a typical major-league baseball season, that translates to thirty-six home runs, 150 RBI and 150 runs scored, not bad for a man not yet old enough to vote. At season's end Seinsoth was named Goldpanner MVP; Boone hit a distant third at .346, although he would be named Goldpanner MVP again in 1968. With Seinsoth and Boone on the Goldpanner roster, there was little likelihood that anyone else would vie for team MVP honors, at least between 1966 and 1968, and no one really did.

For Bill Seinsoth the road to USC and, later on, Fairbanks had been a circuitous one. By the age of ten he had been a seasoned member of the Southern California baseball culture. A veteran Little Leaguer whose reputation for pitching and hitting preceded him, he, along with his friend Dawney, worked as batboys on Bill Sr.'s semipro team, which played its games at Brookside Park in nearby Pasadena, California. Those who watched him scramble from the dugout to home plate and back to the dugout saw something unusual: a gifted pre-teen

Goldpanner star Seinsoth looks tan and fit in Alaska, c. 1967 (*Courtesy of the Goldpanners*)

with enormous physical presence. Not only was he big for his age, but he was strong as an ox and unusually poised for a young boy. Even in his batboy attire, Seinsoth looked every bit the baseball player that some of the men for whom he was retrieving bats did. At that point in his formative years, Bill Seinsoth was a professional baseball player work in progress, a star in the making, even a potential baseball Hall of Famer, some believed. He was tough as nails, too, as he demonstrated by shrugging off a practice pitch that struck him in the head as he stood near the sidelines before one of his father's semipro games—one of many accidents that would befall him. On another occasion he fell off the top of the grandstands. "There were so many close calls," Dauna [Seinsoth] Frazier said (Wagner 2015).

As Seinsoth was growing into the player that others hoped he might become, Justin Dedeaux, then fifteen, was also competing in winter league games at Brookside Park, occasionally against a man thirty years his senior: Bill Seinsoth Sr. Even at his own formative age, Justin Dedeaux was sharp enough to observe the younger Seinsoth with interest, and at some level he must have known he was watching someone with amazing potential and a bright future. Little did he realize that someday

Seinsoth would hit metronomically in leading his father's USC team to an NCAA championship:

> **Bill, Jr., was the batboy, and I'll always remember him because he was so big. He would come out and bounce around the infield and I thought, 'How old is that guy?' He had to be 10 or 11. He'd take infield and he just looked like a ballplayer. I was worried when it came time to recruit him, because we would always bench jockey Bill, Sr. It was good-natured, funny stuff. I thought, maybe Bill, Jr., remembers all that and he thinks SC is a bunch of hot dogs. It turned out he loved us and his dad loved [the bench jockeying] because it was baseball stuff. [My dad] had his eye on Bill, Jr., before he even started high school (Wagner 2015).**

Dedeaux's by then well-known father, Rod, clearly saw the same potential in young Bill Seinsoth, and he began unofficially recruiting the boy at about that time—in the late 1950s. Certainly, it's extraordinary for a renowned college coach—or any college coach—to begin recruiting a youth so early, but Dedeaux was a professional, and he wasn't about to let his protégé, someone whom less astute coaches might not yet consider a solid prospect, slip away. As a result, he kept in contact with both father and son as the younger Seinsoth got bigger and stronger and began to show some serious baseball potential. Here was a real find, Dedeaux must have believed, a diamond in the rough, and the greatest college coach of all time was hopeful of landing him at USC—somehow and someday.

Signing day officially occurred on June 3, 1965, and on June 5—the day after the news media learned the news from the Seinsoth family—local newspapers announced that Arcadia's most favored son was planning to enroll at USC. Young Bill had said it would take a $100,000 bonus to keep him out of college, and he either hadn't received that or wasn't willing to wait to see if such a generous offer would be forthcoming (Jensen 1965). On June 8 the Astros drafted him, but the deal with USC apparently had been sealed. Rod Dedeaux was more than pleased with the young man's decision, as Justin Dedeaux is to this day:

> He was a superstar. From 1968 until he was beaned [the following season] he was as dominating a player as I can recall. He was fierce at the plate and his numbers were huge. He was a great fielder at first base, too, and he had a super arm. He wasn't fast, but he was very agile—he could field the bunts. He was a great athlete.
>
> I would have to say that during that period of my coaching—of course, [former American League Most Valuable Player] Freddie Lynn was fearsome, but this guy was at another level. He hit balls so hard . . . Then, in 1969, his numbers were just huge until he got beaned.
>
> You knew he was going to be a superstar. You knew he was going to be in the big leagues for fifteen or twenty years and probably hit thirty home runs a year. There was no doubt about this guy, there was no doubt about his abilities.
>
> It was clear he was going to be an every-day major-league player. The question was: would he become an all-time great [player], a Hall of Famer? (Wagner 2015).

Freshman coach Merz, at USC from 1965-66, gave all of the credit in recruiting Seinsoth to Rod Dedeaux and the team scouts. As a native of the San Gabriel Valley, where Seinsoth had played his high school ball, Merz was well aware of the young man's credentials and was looking forward to the possibility that USC might be able to land him.

"CIF player of the year—you have to be an idiot [not to be aware of him]," Merz said. "Plus, he was from the San Gabriel Valley, which I stayed in touch with." He added, "I never had any contact with Bill or the family until he got to the campus."

Merz said there was great anticipation for Seinsoth to join the USC baseball program:

> [Signing him] was a coup. He was to become a cornerstone of the franchise, just like a No. 1 draft pick.

Despite his gifts he was absolutely a player who was very well aware of how to handle himself. He was bordering on unassuming. He knew he was good, but he never let you know that he knew he was good. He had that confidence, he was the Natural. There wasn't anything he didn't do very well. He could field, he could run, even for a big-bodied guy. His throwing for a position guy was on target. He was Wes Parker [one of the all-time great fielding first basemen] in the making —his glove was that good.

He hit fourteen bombs [home runs] in 1969 as a senior with a wood bat. As a mature man he might have hit thirty-five or forty home runs more than that. He was run production—whether it was going over the fence or off the wall, runs were going to score. He could get you a base hit, he could hit the other way—he was a smart hitter. He displayed the tools and the wherewithal to use those tools properly.

In the clubhouse he was just another guy, they loved him. He was fun to be around. He was right in the middle of the kidding, even on the freshman team.

How often do players like Bill Seinsoth come along? Merz offered a simple exegesis: "Very infrequently" (Wagner 2015).

To kick-start their varsity careers as well as the 1967 baseball season, Seinsoth and his sophomore-year roommate, Randy Port, a utility player during three seasons at USC, collaborated on a plan to test their skills against each another. One day, the roommates—both had been pitchers in high school—visited Bovard Field after classes were over and threw to each other at full throttle, each batting against the other. According to Port, Seinsoth took the exercise seriously.

"We went out with a bag of balls to see how good we were against each other," Port said. "It was a friendly, competitive thing. Bill['s] first pitch was a fastball right at my head." Port thought to himself, "So this is the way you're going to want to play, huh roomie?" (Wagner 2015).

Port reciprocated by zipping his first pitch directly at Seinsoth's head, and everything was copasetic between the two.

Seinsoth began his sophomore season like the Hall-of-Fame player Justin Dedeaux thought he might someday become—with a bang. He almost had to. After all, the USC baseball media guide inferred future greatness:

> **The best hitting prospect on the freshmen last season, he led the team with .375 mark . . . Drove in 30 runs in 30 games and hit five homers . . . Should start at first . . . Has good size and power, but came to USC with great pitching credentials . . . Won CIF Player of the Year in 1965 at Arcadia High School, where he turned in a 15-1 record as pitcher and played first base . . . Could still pitch and do well . . . Hurled twenty-one innings for frosh with 0.86 E.R.A. and nineteen strikeouts in twenty-one innings . . . Bats and throws left (USC Baseball Media Guide 1965).**

Seinsoth certainly would *not* pitch, and a news release distributed by the Athletic Department explained why in no uncertain terms: Dedeaux wanted him in the starting lineup every day, not just once or twice a week. "Head coach Rod Dedeaux, realizing Seinsoth's potential with the bat, converted the big youngster into a first baseman," it read. Realizing his own potential as a hitter and the depth of the USC pitching staff, Seinsoth offered no argument. "We have a number of good pitchers this season. Runs are what count, and I can hit better than I can pitch," he said (Arnold 1967).

With probably little thought—there was no need for someone with Dedeaux's experience and instincts to give the issue much consideration—the change was made. Seinsoth's overpowering fastball, cool demeanor on the mound, and outstanding earned run average as a freshman notwithstanding, he would not pitch for the Trojans in 1967. Or ever. Unless, of course, a game went long, USC ran out of pitchers, and it was absolutely necessary to use him. That wasn't likely. As Seinsoth indicated, USC was rich with talented, young pitchers, players like future major leaguers Adamson and House. Seinsoth's bat was needed in the lineup, not so much his pitching arm.

House, one of the freshman pitchers brought in along with Seinsoth, was impressive from day one. As a freshman, he was 7-1 with sixty-eight strikeouts in sixty-four innings pitched, recording a 1.40 ERA compared with Seinsoth's brilliant 0.79. After his USC playing days had ended, he was drafted by the Atlanta Braves, where he spent five seasons—his best was 1974 when he went 6-2 with a 1.93 earned run average. He retired in 1978 after eight seasons in the major leagues with twenty-nine wins, twenty-three losses, and a respectable 3.79 ERA.

Adamson, who had arm problems and saw minimal action as a USC freshman, nonetheless pitched well, going 1-1 with a 3.30 ERA and fifteen strikeouts in only eleven innings. However, his tenure at USC was abbreviated. Drafted by the Baltimore Orioles, he signed with the club after his sophomore season as a Trojan, when he was 13-4 with a 1.63 ERA. Adamson spent three years in Baltimore, again suffering arm problems, failing to win a game and posting a 7.46 earned run average before finally calling it quits.

"He had the power, he had a lot of things [necessary] to be a really great baseball player," freshman roommate Adamson said of Seinsoth. "If he had stayed healthy he could have played years in the big leagues" (Wagner 2015).

Like House and Adamson, Seinsoth probably could have made the cut as a top Division I college pitcher—Dedeaux's comments made that abundantly clear in an interview years later. "He had a major-league arm and he was left-handed," the Trojan skipper once said. "And, he was smart" (Wagner 1991).

Seinsoth's other attributes impressed Dedeaux even more, like his six foot two, 220-pound frame and his baseball skill set. "He's got a major-league glove, he's got the moves, and he's definitely got the major-league bat," he said. Adding, "If Bill Seinsoth had lived there's a good chance that no one would have ever heard of Steve Garvey" (Wagner 1991). Coincidentally, both Garvey and Seinsoth would earn American Association of College Baseball Coaches all-America honors in 1968—Seinsoth making the first team and Garvey earning second-team honors.

In typical scheduling fashion, USC began the 1967 campaign playing a mishmash of non-conference games against teams like the Crowley Major League All-Stars, the Los Angeles Dodgers All-Stars, the USC Alumni, and the Philadelphia Phillies All-Stars, with Seinsoth homering against the Phillies All-Stars in the third inning of his seventh varsity game, a 12-11 loss on February 18. Oddly, he would hit only two home runs during the entire season, something that disappointed Seinsoth, who lived and died by the long ball. On March 3 against California State College, Long Beach, he got a taste of the lows of college baseball when, displaying a bit of his father's hot temperament, Seinsoth was ejected in only his eleventh varsity game after arguing an umpire's call. Then things began to turn for the better.

On March 20, in an 8-1 win over San Francisco State College, Seinsoth collected four hits in leading the Trojans to victory. Ten days later he went 2 for 3 with a double and an RBI in a 7-2 victory over Ivy Leaguer Yale. Then he hit a cold streak, failing to get a base hit in consecutive doubleheaders against Washington State and the University of Washington on April 14 and 15, going 0 for 10 over the long, discouraging two days of baseball. The drought continued against Stanford a week later, with Seinsoth going 1 for 6 in a doubleheader, although he did sneak away with a rare stolen base.

As May rolled around, Seinsoth played solidly, slugging a double and a triple in the first game of a doubleheader against Oregon State on May 13 and collecting a single and an RBI in the nightcap. He closed the season going 3 for 7, all of them singles, with two RBI and two runs scored against cross-town rival UCLA.

After a series of ups and downs, Seinsoth's sophomore season was finally in the books, with USC going 9-6 in conference action and 38-13 overall to finish in third place behind Stanford, the league champion, and runner-up UCLA. While his personal numbers had been inglorious compared with previous baseball seasons, they were good enough to lead the Trojans in a couple of important offensive categories. Seinsoth's .327 batting average was the highest on the club, and he tied for the team lead in doubles with eleven. His thirty-one RBI over the fifty-one games ranked third on the ball club, however, his two home runs placed him sixth behind nearly every other starter: only Chuck Ramshaw at shortstop, with none, and Ron Drake at third base, with one, hit fewer home runs as starting-position players. In short, Seinsoth's batting average had been excellent, his doubles and RBI total were fine for a first-year player, but the sum of his home runs had been mediocre. He even pitched two innings in one ballgame, probably out of necessity, striking out two and allowing an earned run to finish the season—and eventually his Trojan career—with a 4.50 ERA. His brief pitching stint aside, there was room for improvement in 1968, and the slugging "savior" with the air of confidence, ever-present smile, and big reputation knew it better than anyone. Despite more bad luck and a physical setback that would knock him out of action for much of 1968, Bill Seinsoth would make his presence known from coast to coast. His performance the next season, one of the most dramatic in college baseball history, would ensure that the name Bill Seinsoth would forever be remembered.

7

BREAKOUT SEASON

"You could tell he was an athlete. When it came time for the [major-league baseball] draft, if someone was going to have a chance to be chosen it was going to be Bill."

–Jim Barr, former pitcher for the San Francisco Giants and California Angels

As spring turns to summer on campuses all across the country, there's nothing more exciting to college-age baseball players than draft day. High-end players wait anxiously and expectantly to learn just how early they'll be chosen, while those with less conspicuous capabilities hope against hope to advance to the next level in their baseball journey. For the highest draft picks, selection by a major-league club often translates to big bonuses and generous salaries. For lower picks, the scenario is much different: the major-league draft is their final chance to live out a lifelong dream, and any salary they might potentially derive if they do end up making the grade pales in importance to their good fortune of actually being chosen in the draft, even at the lower end of the elite.

There's another reality that separates the finest from the not so fine: the general goal of the draft, scouting directors say, is to select the best available talent regardless of either the player's position or the current state of the drafting team, unless, of course, there's a desperate need for a particular type of ballplayer. When draft day 1967 rolled around, the Baltimore Orioles saw some qualities they liked in Seinsoth, and in the June phase of the amateur draft the team selected him in the ninth round as the 155th pick overall. That same season, Baltimore first baseman Boog Powell was twenty-six years old and in the prime of a career that had seen him hit 130 home runs during his first six seasons with the club, although his home run total and RBI production were off significantly that year after an MVP-caliber tour of duty in 1966. Perhaps the Orioles were hedging their bets on Powell, uncertain how the six foot four, 230-pound behemoth might fit into the ball club's future plans. Whatever the reason, Seinsoth, who like Powell was a left-hander with immense power, although with slightly less notable physical dimensions, was a logical hedge.

Powell ended up remaining a significant contributor to the Orioles' fortunes through the 1974 season, earning MVP honors in 1970 and hitting 313 home runs for the club before moving on to Cleveland in 1975 and eventually finishing his career with the Dodgers two years after that. Seinsoth's decision to ultimately forego signing with Baltimore, just as he had done when the Astros drafted him out of high school two years earlier, proved to be the correct one, and he ultimately had no misgivings. One USC teammate took a different approach with the Orioles, however. Chosen by the club in the first round of the draft, which had to please his former roommate Seinsoth, was Adamson, a solid pitcher who was part of the freshman class of ballplayers recruited by Dedeaux. Unfortunately, although Adamson had great potential, it went unfulfilled in a major-league career that began quickly then sputtered due to injury and died a quiet death long before it should have.

With the minimum two years that his father had pledged his son would give USC when he signed to play for the school now behind him, it had become apparent that Seinsoth would return to campus for his third year of eligibility and probably for his senior season as well. By

Seinsoth kneels on deck during a USC game, c. 1968 (*USC Athletics*)

then he was several inches taller than he had been in high school, had gained twenty pounds, had been drafted by two different major-league organizations, and his hoped-for career as a major leaguer was looking more and more likely. He had tasted success both at the freshman and varsity levels of collegiate ball and was looking forward to a breakout season in 1968, with his fellow freshman Trobabes all fully mature and eager to ply their considerable skills in an effort to present Dedeaux with his fifth NCAA championship. Dedeaux, the acme of coaching perfection, as usual expected no less from his team of baseball greyhounds. Neither did Seinsoth expect less from himself, and he set out to prove that his performance in 1967, which many players would have coveted but that he probably considered sub-par, was an aberration.

Bill Seinsoth was a magnet for adversity. Starting in Little League, when the pressure for him to quit because of his dominating skills became withering, scarcely a year went by that he didn't experience a serious injury, life-threatening incident, or both. Bad luck followed him like a dog after kibbles, and a trend was beginning to develop: a fall from the stadium bleachers, driven from Babe Ruth League, the broken noses, all of them in high school, and the slashing, again in high school. The worst was yet to come.

Still, Seinsoth remained insouciant, and his upbeat attitude never appeared to waver. Perhaps he was used to bad luck and considered it his lot in life. Or maybe he figured it came with the territory of being fortunate enough to have skills that would someday reward him handsomely. Whatever the reason, he seldom spoke of the troubling events that seemed to plague him year after year.

One such event occurred sometime during his junior year, probably in late 1967 before baseball season began, after Seinsoth and a female friend entered Baker's Tacos on South Vermont Avenue near the USC campus. At some point during the evening a man with a knife approached the couple, and a threat became imminent. Thinking quickly, Seinsoth ordered his companion to the car and told her to lock herself inside. As he did so, the situation escalated. The man eventually cornered Seinsoth, and for some reason slashed him across the forearm, resulting in a significant loss of blood.

"It was a fairly serious wound," said former teammate Jaffe, adding, "[Baker's Tacos] was not a place where you'd want to be late at night" (Wagner 2015).

Unless, perhaps, you were Bill Seinsoth. Details of the assault remain sketchy to this day, and Seinsoth kept the incident quiet from coaches and most friends—Jaffe is one exception. Seinsoth privately admitted he had been "scared to death," his mother said years later. Justin Dedeaux, his assistant coach at the time, said he had no recollection of the incident, nor did former teammate and close friend House.

"He had to be a pretty stupid guy to pick on somebody Bill's size," House said of the assailant (Wagner 2015).

At least on paper, the Trojans looked superb before the season began, although their schedule had some hot spots. Chief among them were defending Athletic Association of Western Universities Conference (forerunner to the Pacific-8) champion Stanford, which would play the Trojans three times during the season. Also formidable were cross-town rival and always competitive UCLA, which would play the Trojans three times, and two games early on against Brigham Young University, a team that would meet the Trojans for a third time toward the end of the long, drawn out, sixty-five-game schedule—Dedeaux's twenty-seventh at the Trojan helm. California State College, Los Angeles, could also be tough, and the rigorous schedule included three games against the Diablos, since renamed the Golden Eagles. Despite those scheduling challenges, there was always the expectation of winning baseball games.

"[Coach Rod] Dedeaux instilled the fact that we're USC, we win, and we're looking to go to Omaha [and the

Looking chiseled, Seinsoth fields a throw at first base for USC, c. 1968
(*USC Athletics*)

College World Series]," said Seinsoth's teammate Barr, the ex-Giant, "but he never made it an arrogant thing where that's what we had to think about all the time. He would throw it out there, then we would go about our day-to-day business preparing for what we had to do at that time." He added that going to the College World Series "was kind of an expected thing" (Wagner 2015).

The starting lineup that season included a collection of players who were well known among USC baseball watchers, including Steve Sogge at catcher, who was better known as quarterback on the football team and the

In a posed photo, Seinsoth (far left) crouches with fellow USC
starting infielders, c. 1968 (*USC Athletics*)

man who handed the football to Heisman Trophy winner
O. J. Simpson. Others taking the field were Seinsoth at
first base, coming off an MVP summer season with the
Goldpanners despite the presence of future major
leaguers Boone, Jim Nettles, Barr, Lee, and Brent Strom
—the last three of them USC teammates. There was also
future all-American Pat Harrison at second base,
Ramshaw at shortstop, Drake at third base, Pat Kuehner
in left field (and, eventually, at first base replacing
Seinsoth), Jaffe in centerfield, and Reid Braden in right
field. The pitching corps included Barr and the
irrepressible Lee, nicknamed "Spaceman," who would win
119 games during a fourteen-year major-league career
and continued to pitch in the minor leagues into his late
sixties. Lee, a left hander who had won thirteen games for
the Trojans in 1967, and the sophomore Barr, a right-
hander playing his first varsity season, would prove to be
among the finest pitchers in Division I by year end.
Strom, an outstanding pitcher who would throw for the
Mets in the 1970s, along with Bob Vaughn and a host of
others, rounded out Dedeaux's cadre of hurlers.

With rightful anticipation, the Trojans opened the
season on February 7 against the Crowley Major League
All-Stars and nipped them 8-6 at Bovard Field. Opening

day proved to be a good warm-up for the Trojans, and it may have motivated them to step things up a notch. Ten days later, on February 17, Seinsoth demonstrated what his mission would be that season, drilling a three-run home run in the second inning en route to a 4-1 win over the Dodgers rookies, again at Bovard Field. If anything could be said, the big first baseman meant business in 1968, and riding along with him the Trojans opened the season with a 9-1 record.

Then things trailed off dramatically. By the end of March, Seinsoth had hit only three home runs, the third—a two-run blast to right field in the seventh inning—coming in a 9-3 win over Cal State Los

Seinsoth looks toward third base, c. 1968 (USC Athletics)

Angeles on March 26. While the win brought the Trojans' record to 16-6, bad news was just about to strike.

In an April 3 game against Chapman College the cloud that had hung over Seinsoth's head since his Little League days began raining down again, as both he and center fielder Jaffe were struck in the hand by pitched balls. Although USC won the game, 6-2, to improve its record to 20-7, the prognosis was not good for either player, and both appeared to be out for extended periods. At the time, Jaffe was the team's leading hitter at .343, and Seinsoth, the power hitter, was batting cleanup. The student newspaper predicted Jaffe would miss a month of action, while for

Seinsoth the outlook was even more grim: he might be lost for the remainder of the season.

"Seinsoth is probably out for the season," predicted the *Daily Trojan* prematurely (Bales 1968). After the game, doctors confirmed a broken bone in Seinsoth's wrist, and the big first baseman missed the next eighteen games beginning with the week-long Honolulu Invitational Tournament held over Easter, a series of games that Dedeaux obviously took quite seriously despite the exotic venue. "It's a great tourney to be in, and a good vacation," he told one newspaper. "But we're going to Hawaii to play baseball and not to watch the girls in their bikinis" (Troy Wins Game 1968).

Seinsoth demonstrates his batting stance while loosening up before a turn at bat, c. 1968 (*USC Athletics*)

Dedeaux may have misspoke: with injured hands and unable to play, Seinsoth and Jaffe might well have argued they could easily have watched the girls in their bikinis with little negative impact on the team's overall play.

Not long after Seinsoth suffered the injury, sportswriter Dwight Chapin put the Trojans' loss into perspective:

Wanted: left-handed first baseman who is 6-feet-2, weighs 210, can field brilliantly and hit with power. Apply: Rod Dedeaux, USC baseball coach.

Chapin went on to write that without Seinsoth, Dedeaux is only a first baseman shy of being a Pacific-8 title contender, adding the team may be a contender just the same.

> **Seinsoth will have the cast taken off his injured hand next week and Dedeaux is hopeful he can return to action before long.**
> **'With him in there I honestly think we have the finest infield in college baseball,' the Trojan coach said (Chapin 1968).**

During the span of games that Seinsoth was on the bench, USC demonstrated great resilience and an uncanny ability to compensate for the loss of key players. With Kuehner shifted from left field to first base, USC won fourteen games, lost three, and tied one over the eighteen contests that Seinsoth was out of action. USC's record when Seinsoth returned to the field was a healthy 34-10-1, with league play well under way. With the Trojans at full strength, the players were ready to push on toward a league championship and, hopefully, a College World Series berth. They needed Seinsoth, their big gun, to stay healthy the rest of the season if they hoped to advance to post-season play.

"He was such a competitor," Barr said. "Once he walked through that gate at Bovard Field it was all baseball. Bill wanted to be the best athlete he could be, and when a player got on the team he wanted to be just like him" (Wagner 2015).

Seinsoth returned to action May 3 against rival UCLA, making a speedy recovery from his month-long respite to hit a two-run home run in a 7-4 loss. In returning so quickly, he forced the *Daily Trojan* to eat its prediction, made just three weeks earlier, that Seinsoth's season was over: "First baseman Bill Seinsoth made such a rapid recovery from a broken wrist that he hit a two-run homer in the loss to the Bruins," the newspaper backpedaled in a mea culpa (Bales 1968). His wrist obviously healed, Seinsoth proved he wasn't the least bit rusty. From then

Seinsoth, his right wrist wrapped following a serious injury, stands
on second base after returning to action against UCLA, c. 1968

on the Trojans were nearly unbeatable, and Seinsoth
went on a tear. Three games after returning to action with
a home run, Seinsoth went 2 for 3 with another home run
and a single in a 4-3 win over Stanford. The Trojans then
took two from California as Seinsoth went 2 for 5 with an
RBI and two runs scored. In a 10-4 victory over
Washington he went 2 for 4 with a double and an RBI.

Then, in the final game of the regular season against UCLA, Seinsoth doubled, singled, drove in a run, and scored two more to close out conference play with an 11-2 rout of the Bruins. After Seinsoth's return following his wrist injury, USC lost only to Washington State, going 9-1 in the final three weeks of conference play to finish in first place. The big first baseman's return made a huge difference, and as the playoffs began, he was mentally and physically prepared to have an even larger impact.

Moving into the NCAA District 8 playoffs, a prerequisite for the Trojans to compete in the College World Series, USC figured to have a more difficult time, facing a Cal State Los Angeles team that beat USC handily during the regular season. Overall, USC had won two of three games against the Diablos, and taking no chances, Dedeaux started off with ace Lee on the mound. The decision was a propitious one as the Spaceman handcuffed the opposition on eleven hits to pitch a complete game 4-2 win. In that opening game, Seinsoth singled, drove in a run, and had a hand in a rare triple play.

Game two in the best of three series moved to the Diablos' home diamond where the outcome was a marked turnaround from game one. Although Seinsoth doubled and singled in the contest, it wasn't enough, as Cal State topped the Trojans 8-4 in ten innings to force a third and final game, again on Cal State's home field. This time, with Seinsoth drilling two more hits to drive in a run, the Trojans prevailed 5-4 to earn a position at the College World Series. Showing no signs of the mid-season injury that had kept him out of action for a month, Seinsoth went five for eleven in the three-game series against Cal State, batting .454, chipping in two RBI and scoring a run. It was on to Omaha, Nebraska, where few coaches, if any, had more experience —or had experienced more success—than Rod Dedeaux.

★

With his usual spirit of unrestrained confidence, Seinsoth told *Daily Trojan* reporter Jan Arnold prior to the

1968 conference opener that his USC Trojans "could easily be the best team in the nation" (Arnold 1967). The team's performance during the remainder of USC's schedule lent credence to that claim. As the Trojans prepared for BYU and their first-round game in the College World Series, it was looking very much like Seinsoth knew exactly what he was talking about. Still, BYU was no slouch, and the Cougars had split the two games they played against USC prior to league play, blanking the Trojans on a pitching gem, 7-0, then losing in a shutout themselves, 3-0. Their first meeting in Omaha would be anybody's ballgame, and Coach Dedeaux understood that better than most people. His teams had played in the finals five times previously during his illustrious coaching career, and although he had won four NCAA championships, Dedeaux *had* tasted defeat on one occasion, losing to Minnesota in 1960. Having both won and lost in the coveted College World Series finals, Dedeaux knew that no elite team, certainly no team good enough to earn a trip to the tournament, could be taken for granted, and BYU was no exception. He also knew how to get the most out of his high-octane group of players. "Coach Dedeaux makes baseball fun," Seinsoth said. "I really think he can perfect almost every aspect of any player's game" (Seinsoth's Goal Is 1967). At that point it was time for Barr, Lee, Seinsoth, and their blue-chip teammates to bring forward the skills that Dedeaux had perfected. All three, along with the rest of the squad, were prepared to do just that. However, in the most important series of his career, Bill Seinsoth would go a step further, playing perhaps the finest ball of his life, and folks reading about him in newspapers around the country would take notice. In the '68 Series, Seinsoth, now fit, focused, and ready to play for keeps, was the man of the hour for Dedeaux and his Trojans, and he knew just what he had to do to make an NCAA championship happen. To those around the country observing the greatest college baseball spectacle of all, that hour and those games, against the toughest competition college baseball had to offer, would mark the high point of Bill Seinsoth's brilliant career up until that point, a high-water mark that would stand the test of time. Unfortunately, time for Bill Seinsoth was running out.

8

NATIONAL CHAMPIONS

"He knew he was good, but he never let you know that he knew he was good. He had that confidence, he was the Natural. There wasn't anything he didn't do very well. He was Wes Parker in the making."

¬Jerry Merz, former freshman baseball coach at USC, former pitcher in the Cincinnati Reds and San Francisco Giants organizations

If youth is squandered on the young, then Bill Seinsoth was born old. In his athletically charged life, Seinsoth had never wasted a single moment, excelling at everything he put his mind to. His propensity to excel was magnified in sports, and his accomplishments were fast accumulating. His high school team had won the equivalent of a state title, and Seinsoth was named player of the year. He also was MVP for the elite Alaska Goldpanners in the summer of 1967, leading a team that included several future major leaguers. He led the freshman team at USC in pitching (ERA) and hitting (batting average). And now he was guiding the varsity in its quest for an NCAA title. As the College World Series began at spacious Johnny Rosenblatt Stadium in Omaha, Nebraska, a ballpark that opened the year Seinsoth was born, the stage was set for something special to occur. The only question was, could Seinsoth and his teammates capitalize?

Joining USC and BYU in the postseason tournament were an eclectic group of college teams, ranging from Ivy

Leaguer Harvard, making its first appearance in the spring classic, to powerhouse Texas, which recruited Seinsoth in high school and had appeared in the tournament nine times previously. Half of the eight teams in the single-elimination tournament had never before competed in the College World Series, and rounding out the list of qualifiers were Southern Illinois, North Carolina State, Oklahoma State (making its seventh appearance), and St. John's (third appearance). Like Texas, USC was also making a tenth appearance in the tournament, its first since 1966 when it lost in the semifinals. Among the participants in 1968 only USC, Texas, and Oklahoma State had previously won NCAA baseball titles.

Reading Joe Hendrickson's column in the *Pasadena Independent*, it's easy to assume that most people believed the College World Series was Dedeaux's to lose, and perhaps it was. Describing him as "a trucking magnate who coaches baseball as a hobby," Hendrickson also called Dedeaux, who founded multimillion-dollar DART Transportation, "the silent mayor of Omaha," "the czar of the NCAA," and "the victory king of USC."

"It shows what a man can do when he doesn't have to win for a living," he wrote. "Dedeaux coaches because it gives him something to play with besides money—and he coaches well." Then Hendrickson turned his attention to one of the products of Dedeaux's good coaching: his multi-talented first baseman Bill Seinsoth, who soaked up instruction like a bee does pollen.

"Somebody always comes along to pick us up," he quoted Dedeaux. "Bill Seinsoth of Arcadia rejoined the team after recovering from a broken hand just in time to help us knock out UCLA." Hendrickson then described Seinsoth as "a big, strong first baseman . . . considered another major-league futurity" (Hendrickson 1968). For Seinsoth, his "futurity" was now.

Just as things appeared to be on track for the top-seeded Trojans, tragedy struck off the field. Only days before USC was scheduled to leave for Omaha, starting left fielder Pat Kuehner's eighteen-year-old brother, Tim, was killed in an automobile accident in Orange County, California. Kuehner skipped the team flight in order to attend his brother's funeral, then chartered a private airplane, flew to Omaha, changed into his Trojan uniform while riding to Rosenblatt Stadium in the back seat of a USC supporter's car, and arrived at the ballpark thirty minutes before play was to begin against BYU—only to strike out on three consecutive pitches in the first inning. "Where am I, what am I doing here?" he privately wondered (Wagner 2015). Kuehner would wonder that many times over the next four games, as he failed to collect a base hit in his first fourteen at bats.

What a week it had been for the young man. Within a span of just four days Kuehner lost his brother, was chosen in the major-league draft by the Washington Senators, missed the team flight to Omaha, attended his brother's funeral, then hustled to Omaha in time to make the starting lineup against BYU later that day, going hitless in four at bats. His world was a blur of time, space, and events as well as a mix of emotions, both exceedingly good and unthinkably bad. Understandably distracted, unable to get a base hit, and probably exhausted both emotionally and physically, he wouldn't have missed the series for the world.

"Skipping the series was never a consideration," he said. "Once I got back there I tried to get focused, but obviously I was not as focused as I should have been" (Wagner 2015).

Against BYU, Kuehner wasn't the only Trojan having trouble focusing. USC collected just two base hits in the team's June 11 opener, including a single by Seinsoth. However, they managed to capitalize on a pair of walks, a hit batter, an error, and a sacrifice fly to score five runs

Pat Kuehner, hero of the 1968 College World Series, kneels for a
photographer (*USC Athletics*)

and beat the Cougars 5-3. Lee picked up his twelfth win
on the season, going the distance and striking out eight
batters.

The following day the Trojans came back against Oklahoma State and had better luck at the plate, although the outcome was even closer than the day before. With Barr, who was 10-2 on the year, and Bob Vaughn, 9-4, battling arm problems late in the season (OSU Falls 1968), Dedeaux elected to pitch Jim Southworth in Game 2, however, the Cowboys came out on fire, scoring four runs in the bottom of the first inning after the Trojans had taken a 1-0 lead in the top half. Down 4-1 after only an inning, Dedeaux removed Southworth, and Brent Strom came on to pitch eight innings of brilliant relief for USC, striking out eleven batters and leading the Trojans to a 6-5 second-round win. Although the team picked up six hits in the game to give them a still-scant eight during the first two rounds, Seinsoth went hitless in three at bats against OSU—the only game in which he would not hit safely.

In the quarterfinal round the following day, USC again had its hands full, this time against St. John's, but the hitting was beginning to come around. John Rockwell started the game on the mound for the Trojans and was relieved by Lee in the third inning, with neither pitcher allowing a run before Barr came on in the fourth to go the rest of the way. Seinsoth picked up two hits, including a double, as the Trojans overcame a 6-2 deficit to knock off the Redmen, 7-6, scoring the tie-breaking run in the eighth inning.

Desperately in need of a breather, USC's fourth game in four days would not provide it. Hoping to save Lee for the finale—if his team was able to get that far—Dedeaux started Vaughn against North Carolina State, and although he pitched a complete game shutout, the victory didn't come easily. In collecting eight hits, including another double and a single by Seinsoth, the Trojans scored once in the fourth and once in the fifth to notch the win and give Vaughn the 2-0 victory. It was on to the finals for USC and a chance to win another NCAA baseball title.

★

In four games the Trojans had won three times by a single run, and if anything could be said about their play, it was that USC made its cruise through the playoffs appear surprisingly difficult. As expected, the pitching had been solid, but the team's hitting was desultory—in four playoff games the Trojans had collected just twenty-five hits, an average of only six per game. USC, which hit four home runs for every five games played during the regular season, had connected for only one round tripper thus far—Harrison's blast against St. John's in the quarterfinals. Even more ominous, in three of the four playoff victories USC had to come from behind to win. The Trojans would need to do better if they hoped to beat a tough Southern Illinois University squad on June 15, their fifth game in five days.

"I don't think I was the only one not hitting," Kuehner said, adding that, "Bill [Seinsoth] was kind of carrying us. It was very frustrating. The major frustration was when I found out I wasn't going to be playing in the final game"— or so he thought (Wagner 2015).

As the starting lineups for the championship game against the Southern Illinois Salukis were announced, one name was noticeably missing from the Trojan card: Kuehner. Ineffective as a hitter in four consecutive playoff games, Kuehner would not start in the biggest game of his life, replaced in left field by Bill Homik, who although having batted only thirty-three times during the regular season was hitting an impressive .432 at game time. Dedeaux needed some punch in left field, and with a left-hander starting, Homik, who had muscled three home runs and two doubles on the season and had seventeen hits, was the preferred choice to start (Shadle 1968). Kuehner admitted, "I probably should have been benched earlier" (Wagner 2015).

The starting pitcher that day was the Spaceman, Bill Lee, and in case the Trojan ace got into trouble, the

formidable Brent Strom was waiting in the wings to help
him out. There was trouble from the outset. SIU center
fielder Jerry Bond led off the game with a double and
quickly came home on a single by right fielder Mike
Rogodzinski. Another run in the third inning made it 2-0,
but by the fourth the Trojans came back with two of their
own on a single by Kuehner's replacement, Homik, and a
booming home run that Seinsoth drilled over the right
field fence. SIU pulled ahead in the eighth on an infield
hit and an overthrow, followed by a walk, a force play at
second, and a single. That set the stage for perhaps the
greatest comeback story to any game in College World
Series history.

Leading off for the Trojans in the bottom of the ninth
inning was Reid Braden, who walked and went to second
on a single by Seinsoth. With two on, the third baseman
Drake forced his slow-footed first baseman out at second
on a ground ball to short. Pinch hitter Rich McCombs
then hit a shot toward second that struck Drake as he
tried to move up, and Drake was called out.

With two out in the bottom of the ninth, losing by a
run with two runners on, USC's back was up against the
wall. The team needed a miracle to tie the game and an
even bigger one to win it, with the pitcher Strom coming
to the plate. Strom, who was batting .158 on the season,
would not hit. Instead, Dedeaux surveyed his bench
looking for someone who could provide some badly
needed pop. His eyes fixed on Kuehner.

Kuehner was zero for everything in the tournament,
but he had played solidly during the regular season.
Although his batting average was only .235, he did have
two home runs, two triples, and eleven doubles. At that
point, Dedeaux just needed a single to tie the game, and a
double or triple would win it. Kuehner was capable of any
kind of hit.

At that moment, Kuehner's thoughts had to be
jumbled. While mourning the recent loss of his brother, he

had been anemic at the plate, had not started in the most important—and final—game of his college career, was on the verge of watching his last shot at an NCAA championship wither into dust, and the greatest coach in college baseball history was now looking his way for help. With what probably seemed like a desperation move to anyone aware of Kuehner's difficulties, Dedeaux, puissant and in control, walked the dugout until he reached Kuehner, then stopped and recited a familiar line. Kuehner had heard it before, as had other Trojans: "Grab your gun, tiger, we've got one left and you're it" (Wagner 2015).

Kuehner's gun was his bat, and as he walked to the plate the world was on his shoulders. Not only was the NCAA championship on the line, but how he did in his final collegiate at bat would be remembered, most certainly by himself and his teammates, for decades to come. Based upon his previous fourteen at bats, the odds were long that Kuehner would deliver, especially facing a left-hander. Or did his zero for 14 series make him long overdue for a base hit? Dedeaux apparently believed it did.

With runners on first and third and facing SIU relief pitcher Skip Pitlock, who was known for his unorthodox pitching delivery, Kuehner watched a fastball go by for a strike. Pitlock then threw another strike past him, rekindling memories of Kuehner's first at bat in game one against BYU when he struck out on three straight pitches. The question in Kuehner's mind at that point was what would Pitlock come back with—a fastball or a curve? Announcer Dave Blackwell set the table:

> **No balls, two strikes, two outs, bottom half of the ninth inning, 3-2 Southern Illinois leading, Southern Cal at bat, Kuehner up, runners on first and third, and Skip Pitlock gets ready for this all-important pitch. He looks in for the sign . . . (Blackwell 1968).**

According to Kuehner, the USC scouting report indicated that Pitlock did not like to throw his curve with runners on third base, because he tended to bounce the ball. "I'm thinking, 'I hope that scouting report is right, because if he throws that big overhand curveball I'm dead,'" Kuehner said. "If he throws the curveball I'm probably 0 for 15" (Wagner 2015).

Pitlock played it safe, perhaps too safe. He came back with another fastball and Kuehner was waiting for it, drilling the ball with a big swing deep to right-centerfield toward the 375-feet mark.

As the ball took off, reality became "a little bit of a blur" to Kuehner, although he later saw on replays that it sailed over the outfielder's head and hit the wall about a foot from the top. "I hit it pretty solid, and I looked up hoping to get it over their heads," he said. "It was way over their heads." Announcer Blackwell continued with the dramatic story:

> **Swung on, and there's a long, long fly, way back and it's off the wall. One run is in . . . and it looks like Southern Cal has won the championship. Unbelievable! Absolutely unbelievable (Blackwell 1968)!**

Braden trotted in from third, and McCombs took off from first as Kuehner began running. Within seconds, the game was over, and USC had won the national championship 4-3 on the strength of its unlikeliest hero: Pat Kuehner. Dedeaux's decision to send Kuehner in as a pinch hitter turned from questionable to brilliant in one stroke of the bat.

In the moments that followed, with the crowd roaring, members of the Trojan team carried Kuehner off the field on their shoulders. A widely circulated wire service photo showed a jubilant Kuehner riding high above the player whose home run had tied the score in the fourth inning and whose single had enabled Braden to get into scoring position and eventually tie the game before McCombs pushed the Trojans ahead. Bill Seinsoth's fingers were extended in a "V" for victory. Following his team's sixty-fifth game of the season, Seinsoth, who seemed ubiquitous during the five games, was named College World Series most outstanding player, receiving a commemorative watch that blinked "MVP" several times each minute. (A classmate said that in time Seinsoth learned exactly how many steps he could take in between blinks.) Joining him on the all-tournament team was Lee, who at 12-3 finished his Trojan season with a sterling 1.99 ERA.

Lee was a rare teammate who was ever able to find a flaw in Seinsoth's play, other than his slowness of foot. That shortcoming, said Lee, who as a pitcher admitted he was always looking for faults in hitters—even his own hitters—was his inability to hit high pitches.

"He was very susceptible to a high fastball after you started him out with breaking balls," he said of Seinsoth, who paradoxically would strike out only twenty-five times in 175 at bats the next season. Lee then offered a caveat: "Bill was unbelievable. He could crush everything at certain times." Goldpanner teammate Boone propounded that the fastball issue was something Seinsoth would have adapted to: "Certainly. [That was] pretty typical for left-hand hitters. [They are] low-ball hitters" (Wagner 2015).

The high fastball shortcoming, as Lee perceived it, didn't seem to affect Seinsoth's success in the 1968 College World Series, where he was the only regular Trojan player to hit over .300.

"We didn't hit well the entire tournament," Kuehner told reporters after the game. "Except for Billy Seinsoth, we didn't have another player with more than three hits in the tournament" (Trojans' Comeback 1968). Kuehner misspoke: Harrison, Braden, and Drake all had four hits while Seinsoth, with two hits in three of the five games, had seven.

At last, after years of painstaking dedication, Seinsoth had reached a pinnacle as, arguably, the greatest college baseball player in the world, recording a .389 batting average for the series with one home run, two doubles, and four singles. The boy from Arcadia, who was forced from Little League and Babe Ruth League by people who complained he was too good, had proved them correct. Bill Seinsoth *was* too good—*way* too good.

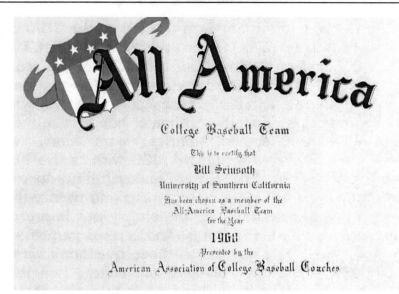

Seinsoth's 1968 All-America certificate still hangs in Rod Dedeaux's former office, which is now an archive for USC baseball. (*Rod Dedeaux archives*)

"It seems like only a couple of weeks ago that we watched Bill pitch Arcadia into the CIF championships with a 15-1 senior season mound performance—earning CIF player of the year honors on the way," wrote one scribe two days after USC's dramatic one-run victory in the College World Series. "Now, he's a 6-2, 220-pound first baseman, the top hitter in the Pac-8 this past season as a junior, and a good bet to be the most sought after collegiate player in the nation when he finishes up his USC career next spring." In a sophistic footnote, he added, "Keep an eye on this young man. He's going to make his mark in the 'bigs'" (Pickard 1968).

While deservedly the tournament's most valuable player, several questions remained unanswered. Why, for instance, did Seinsoth fail to make the All-Pacific-8 Conference team even though he led the league in batting with a .429 average? Six of his teammates made the team (nine Trojans signed contracts to play professionally). Was it because he missed eighteen games due to the broken wrist, eight of them against Pacific-8 opponents? In all, he missed nearly half of the conference games that USC played. And why did he not earn a berth on the NCAA All-District 8 first team, or even the second team? His absence from play for more than a quarter of the season didn't seem to matter to the American Association of College Baseball Coaches or to the Sporting News, which both bestowed on him the ultimate honor when they named him to their all-America team along with teammate Harrison, who had led USC with twelve home runs and forty-seven RBI. Or were his overall numbers—a .312 batting average with six home runs and twenty-three RBI in the games he did play in—simply not impressive enough, even though the injury and missed games were largely responsible? Answers to those questions weren't important. With one season of college eligibility remaining, Seinsoth had nothing more to prove. He had risen to the top, playing superbly at every point along the way and receiving all of the major honors, including all-America and College World Series most outstanding player. The only goal left for him to accomplish was winning a second consecutive NCAA championship. Or, having been picked in the fifth round (ninety-fifth overall) by the Dodgers in the June secondary phase of the baseball draft that was held three days before the College World Series began, would Seinsoth leave college to pursue a career in professional baseball? His decision was announced, at least privately, while he waited for representatives of the Dodgers to interview him at Dodger Stadium. As he sat impatiently, a door opened in the front office and out walked Dedeaux. It was then that the young acolyte told his skipper he would return to USC for his senior season, a decision that had to delight his teammates and coaches while disappointing the Dodgers. The reason for that decision was Dedeaux himself, whom Seinsoth had known since his childhood and whose instruction and encouragement throughout the years he had grown to treasure.

"I guess I felt I owed something to Dedeaux," Seinsoth told a reporter, calling his decision "kind of a sentimental thing, I guess. After going this far I thought I should finish. I'll graduate on schedule [next] June" (Garrett 1969). Loyal to the end, Seinsoth wasn't about to disappoint the man who had guided him along by leaving the program early. His honesty was refreshing, and his willingness to pass up what might amount to a six-figure, major-league bonus out of appreciation for his college coach was even more refreshing. There would be many years to enjoy the fruits of a major-league baseball career, or so Seinsoth thought, but he only had one more year of college eligibility remaining, just one year during which to learn as much as possible from the iconoclastic Dedeaux, and Seinsoth was prepared to stick around. The unique partnership between USC baseball, Rod Dedeaux, and Bill Seinsoth wasn't quite over.

9

KNOCKDOWNS AND NICETIES

*"It was a bad beaning. I wouldn't have blamed him if
he had backed off after that. But he adjusted just
beautifully. He adjusted to everything."*
–Rod Dedeaux, former head baseball coach at USC

With a 4-0 win over the Yakima Indians, Seinsoth wrapped
up his regular season Goldpanner career on July 30,
1968, with a single in two plate appearances. The previous
night he had returned to the lineup for the first time since
stepping on a baseball and spraining his ankle, probably
prior to a game against the Bellingham Bells on July 17.
His return to the lineup two weeks after the injury was a
day late and a dollar short for the big first baseman. The
night before, Al Campanis, who was then head of the
Dodgers' scouting department but would move into the
general manager position later that year, was at the game
to watch Seinsoth and the team's other draftees play. He
must have left disappointed at not being able to see his
presumed first baseman of the future in action.

At the close of the regular season, the Goldpanners
would embark on a two-week exhibition tour of Japan in
early August, and the final mention of Bill Seinsoth in
Goldpanner flannels occurred on August 12, 1968, in the
Fairbanks News-Miner: "First baseman Bill Seinsoth of
the University of [Southern] California smashed a two-
out, two-run homer in the fourth inning to give the

ALASKA
GOLDPANNERS
of Fairbanks

"HOME OF MIDNIGHT SUN BASEBALL"

OFFICIAL PROGRAM

BOB BOONE
Third year with club. Batted .346 last year
after leading the team in 1967 with a .368
average. Plays third base.

BILL SEINSOTH
Third year with club. Batted .382 last year
to lead team in hitting. Smashed 12 home
runs. Plays first base.

Alaska Goldpanners team program features future major-league all-star Bob Boone and Seinsoth, from 1968 (*Courtesy of the Goldpanners*)

Americans a 2-0 lead" (in a game they eventually lost, 5-2, to a Sumitomo Metal Industries team) (Fairbanks News-Miner 1968), it read. The home run seemed like a fitting way for Seinsoth's Goldpanner career to wind down —he hit twenty-three home runs during his three years in

Fairbanks, and it was nice to approach the finish line on a high note after the injury. Several days later the Goldpanners would cancel a planned trip to the National Baseball Congress post-season tournament in Wichita, Kansas, citing illness to several team members that apparently arose during the team's tour of Japan. When the Japan tour ended, Seinsoth's three-summer Goldpanner career was over, and his final-season statistics, while good enough for most ballplayers, probably disappointed him, at least a little: a .327 batting average with five HR and twenty-seven RBI. Good friend Bob Boone was named team MVP, as he had been in 1966 the year before Seinsoth won the honor, and Seinsoth's focus quickly turned to his senior year at USC and his final season of NCAA eligibility.

In January 1969, a month before USC's opening day, Rod Dedeaux named Seinsoth, whom teammate Craig Perkins called "the pillar of the team," captain for that season. "After leading the Pacific-8 in hitting with a robust .429 mark, he is considered a top all-America candidate this year," wrote the *Daily Trojan* in announcing the appointment. "And, he turned down a pro offer to return to Troy for 1969" (Seinsoth Baseball Captain 1969). In the team photo for that season a broadly smiling Seinsoth is seated at Dedeaux's immediate left, an honor reserved for the leader of the team. As the season progressed, Seinsoth proved that the honor was more than symbolic. By the time the season was over, he would either lead the team or tie for the lead in games played, runs, hits, doubles, triples, home runs, and RBI—every meaningful offensive category.

Unlike 1968 when his home run total of six was well below expectations, 1969 proved to be a long ball year for the aggressive—the *Tribune* called him "hard-nosed" (Don't Forget Young Billy 1969)—Seinsoth, and the boost in offensive production satisfied him. In the second game of the season against a team of Los Angeles Dodgers rookies, he blasted a two-run home run to give USC a 3-2 victory and post an exclamation point on his intentions

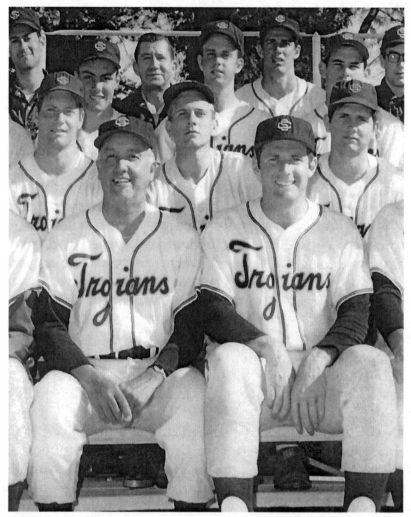

USC's 1969 team photo shows Seinsoth, the captain, seated next to legendary coach Rod Dedeaux (*USC Athletics*)

for 1969. The following game he hit a solo shot in a win over San Fernando Valley State College. After that the home runs came fast and furious. "Seinsoth's Home Run Sparks Troy Victory," read a March 29 headline following a win over Pepperdine College. The next day a headline upped the ante in a win over BYU, reading, "Seinsoth Homers (two) Spark Trojans." Then, on April 19, a headline read "Seinsoth Leads Trojans in Split" as the USC slugger hit a grand slam and a solo home run in a doubleheader against Washington State. Hitting with abandon, he was wearing down pitchers left and right, and it had to be an annoyance to the opposition.

"This is the first year I've really had any understanding of what I was doing as a hitter," said the big all-American. "Now, I can stand in the batting cage and I know if I'm doing something wrong, and I can correct it. I never could do that before. I'm much more relaxed at the plate" (Garrett 1969).

Perhaps too relaxed. Seinsoth's proclivity to hit for power came to a crashing halt two days later on April 21 in a doubleheader against Oregon State when tragedy struck again. After belting a two-run homer and a single in the opener against the Beavers, his twelfth blast of the season to drive in his forty-sixth and forty-seventh runs, Seinsoth came to bat in the first inning of the nightcap against pitcher Lloyd Wilson, a six foot two left hander. He confidently dug in against Wilson, who promptly delivered a fastball that struck him flush over the right eye, sending him sprawling.

"He was unconscious for quite some time," his mother recalled years later.

With his horrified dad seated in the stands and looking on, Seinsoth was carried from the field and transported to USC Medical Center, where he required fifteen stitches to close a gaping laceration above his eye. He was held overnight for observation in the USC infirmary, then re-examined the following day.

"I saw him the next morning and I couldn't even tell he had a face, it was so swollen," his mother said (Wagner 1991).

Never prone to exaggeration, Seinsoth described the incident nonchalantly to the *Daily Trojan* that same day. "I saw the pitch, then lost it," he said of the fastball, described as a brush-back pitch by the newspaper. "The ball came pretty hard" (Seinsoth Sees Trojan Win 1969).

The day after his injury, with Seinsoth in the infirmary, USC beat Oregon 5-1. In a performance that had to make him proud, Seinsoth's closest friend on the

Seinsoth smiles confidently while awaiting his turn to bat for the Trojans, 1969 (USC Athletics)

team, Buzz Shafer, played first base for his pal and doubled his first time at bat.

After the beaning, Seinsoth suffered a blood clot behind the eye as well as split vision, where half the field of vision in one or both eyes was missing. He remained undaunted after foregoing the game against Oregon and was looking forward to a pair of contests against Stanford and Cal the following weekend.

"There may be a problem of double vision, but I hope not," he said. "I think I'll be all right. I don't know if I'll play this weekend, but I should be in a position to see some action. I wouldn't miss those games for the world" (Seinsoth Sees Trojan Win 1969).

Dedeaux was also hopeful, although noncommittal. "He's sure he can play," he told the *Daily Trojan*, "but we'll have to wait and see. He can't open his eye all the way right now, but his vision is 100 percent perfect. Without him in the lineup it makes a great difference. He's one of college baseball's best hitters." The newspaper noted, "Seinsoth was in good spirits as he left with his teammates for the Bay Area yesterday—wearing sunglasses and promising to uphold the traditions of Dedeaux Island" (a traffic island in San Francisco where Dedeaux and his team traditionally visited when in town). "Part of that tradition, of course, is winning" (Swegles 1969).

As it turned out, Seinsoth did see action the following weekend. In the Trojans' third game since the beaning, Seinsoth banged out two singles in the nightcap of a doubleheader against Cal, although USC lost the game 5-4. After suffering a horrible beaning on a Monday, Seinsoth was back in hitting form five days later.

"It was a bad beaning," recalled Rod Dedeaux years after the incident. "I wouldn't have blamed him if he had backed off after that. But he adjusted just beautifully. He adjusted to everything" (Wagner 1991).

Aggressive as ever, Bill Seinsoth was back. His return didn't surprise 1968 College World Series hero Kuehner, who knows something about coming back from adversity.

"He was so aggressive as a hitter, which you have to be [in order] to be a good hitter," said Kuehner. "He almost hit left-handed pitchers as good as or better than right-handers. It's a difficult thing as a lefty to hang in there against a good lefty, and Bill was probably the best I'd ever seen at that. It's not unusual that he would take a shot [to the head] like that because he hit lefties very, very well" (Wagner 2015).

It may not have been unusual, but it was not something he was willing to have repeated. Later that season, Seinsoth reacted with a rare display of anger when a teammate fatuously lobbed a ball toward his head. No one, he admonished, would ever again throw at his head.

After the beaning, Seinsoth's home-run production dropped off dramatically. He had hit twelve in the first thirty-seven games, and in the last fifteen after returning to the lineup he hit just two. Despite the drop-off in home run production, he finished the season with a .368

Seinsoth follows through on a picture-perfect swing for the Trojans, c. 1969 (*USC Athletics*)

batting average overall as USC ended Pac-8 play in third place behind UCLA and Washington State. Anyone would have been happy with a .368 batting average, and even Seinsoth had to be satisfied considering the shot he took to his eye: although his batting average was down twenty-one points after the beaning, it still marked the highest average in his four years at USC. His fourteen home runs were among the NCAA leaders.

In his final game as a Trojan, perhaps to show his spunk or maybe to leave his mark at USC, the usually controlled Seinsoth was ejected from a ballgame against UCLA for unknown reasons. Fittingly, so was Dedeaux, who like Seinsoth was also forced to leave the premises. Dedeaux returned to observe the rest of the game seated in the stands—disguised as a woman.

That was Seinsoth's swan song, and Mike Ball, who replaced him in the lineup after his ejection, promptly hit a home run to underscore that the guard would be changing. The following season and for five consecutive years, Dedeaux would lead the Trojans to College World Series titles—a record unmatched either before or since. With Seinsoth departing, there would be new stars joining the team—names like Fred Lynn and Steve Kemp—another Arcadian. In 1969 there would be no NCAA championship for the Trojans, the only time they would not win a title over a seven-year span that began in 1968. Seinsoth would have to be content with the team's 41-12 record and a third-place finish in the Pac-8 Conference. Despite his heroic offensive numbers, Seinsoth failed to capture either all-conference or all-America honors.

Not long after the season unofficially ended, the Trojans played an exhibition game in nearby Commerce, California. During the game Jaffe hit an opposite-field home run. Afterward, as Jaffe said good-bye to his teammate for what would be the last time, Seinsoth shook his head good-naturedly and said to the lefty, "How can *you* hit a home run to left field?" (Wagner 2015). Jaffe never saw his friend again.

Former Bakersfield teammate Tom Paciorek, who played eighteen years in the major leagues, including six seasons with the Los Angeles Dodgers, recalled that Seinsoth himself could hit the ball to left field when he wanted to, something that requires both strength and skill. "It seemed like he hit everything to the opposite field," he said. "He had extra base power. Obviously, the scouts thought he was gonna be [good]." Paciorek added, "He was one of those guys who was real confident in his ability. I think that's great" (Wagner 2015). Like Seinsoth, Paciorek was a first-team all-American in 1968.

To Seinsoth, the failure to qualify for post-season play in 1969 was probably just as well. He would tell a reporter in August 1969 that he was "psychologically worn out after just graduating in June. I need a month's vacation right now" (Marin 1969). That wouldn't happen. Bill Seinsoth's days as a Trojan baseball player may have been over, but there was no time to relax and unwind before turning his attention to bigger and better things.

The question was, with his Goldpanner and USC careers over, where would he play baseball next? His decision would please everyone.

10

DODGER BLUE

"[Bill Seinsoth] was the leading candidate to replace Wes Parker. He really had a good future in front of him" (Wagner 1991).

–Ben Wade, former director of scouting for the
Los Angeles Dodgers

When the secondary phase of major-league baseball's June amateur draft rolled around, there were probably big questions around the USC athletic department: which team would select Seinsoth, and in which round? Certainly, Southern Californians were hoping the Dodgers would draft him, and such a move would make sense. Dodgers first baseman Wes Parker, who was then only twenty-nine, would play another three seasons with the club. However, some in the organization probably sensed it was time to enlist the services of another, younger first baseman in advance of Parker's eventual retirement, someone who could hit the long ball with more consistency than Parker, yet field with similar adeptness. The team had Steve Garvey on its roster, but at that point he was a third baseman who had difficulty making the long throw across the infield. Ron Fairly was in his final year with the team, and by then he was only playing first base part time. Seinsoth's cousin, Tommy Hutton, had seen minimal action with the team as a first sacker and in fact would not play again for the major-league club after 1969. One prospect was Paciorek. The future all-star, who could hit for power, would join the Dodgers in 1970 and play six seasons with the team, but Paciorek didn't catch on as a regular first baseman. Someone was needed who could step in when Parker, who would win his third of six Gold Glove awards that season, was ready to hang up his cleats.

Earlier in 1969 Seinsoth had been picked by the Washington Senators in the fourth round of the secondary phase of baseball's January draft. Just as he had when drafted earlier by the Astros, Orioles, and most recently by the Dodgers in 1968, Seinsoth didn't sign. At the time, he was committed to finishing his career at USC and nothing short of Dedeaux's retirement could change that, not even a contract with the Senators, who at that time were managed by someone who could teach Seinsoth the intricacies of hitting like no one else: Ted Williams.

Seinsoth's commitment not to sign ended in the spring of 1969 when the Trojans finished out of the money in the Pacific-8 Conference. With his college years over, it was time for Seinsoth to take the baseball draft more seriously. On June 5, when the Dodgers picked him in the first round of the June amateur draft as the team's no. 8 selection overall, Seinsoth had to be pleased.

So, too, were Dodgers fans. Here was a big, tall, home-grown, home run hitter with personality, character, good looks, and charisma, and as a local boy he was looking forward to eventually playing every day in front of his friends and family. Not to mention the USC family, which was well represented throughout the bustling, baseball-savvy Los Angeles area. If all went as hoped, Seinsoth could be playing for the big club by 1970 or 1971, and that would be fine by him.

It was fine by his family, too. As things progressed it was looking more and more like Bill Sr. would finally get to watch his son do something he himself had dreamed of doing—play in a major-league game. If things continued along as they were, the elder Seinsoth might be able to watch his son play regularly at Dodger Stadium or even on television from the comfort of his own armchair in the family's Arcadia home. Everything was finally falling into place.

"There was no one ahead of him," recalled the late Ben Wade, longtime director of scouting for the Dodgers and the man who signed Seinsoth on June 9, 1969. "He was always a good power hitter, and that's one of the things you're looking for—especially a left-handed hitter. With his tools and his success in college he really had a good future in front of him.

"I would have to say he was the leading candidate [to replace Wes Parker]" (Wagner 1991).

On June 10, 1969, the *Pasadena Star-News*, which had closely followed Seinsoth's career since his high school days, announced his signing with the Dodgers, which occurred the day after his college graduation, with a headline that read, simply: "Seinsoth Signed." The kicker headline read, perhaps prophetically, "New Dodger slugger!" The newspaper, which indicated Seinsoth had signed for between $10,000 and $15,000, said he had been assigned to Bakersfield, in the California League.

In a subsequent interview, Seinsoth played coy about the contract. "It is a good deal, the best I could have received," he said. "I am very happy" (Pineda 1969).

The numbers that the *Star-News* published may have been off by more than a little. Others have reported that the big first baseman had signed for a bonus of $40,000. Whatever the sum, after some obligatory seasoning he would return to Los Angeles to play for the next ten, fifteen, or even more years, many believed. Bill Seinsoth was going to be a Los Angeles Dodger someday, perhaps very soon, and that was that.

"We are very happy to get him," said Al Campanis, then a Dodgers vice president and head of scouting. "He was our No. 1 draft choice last year and we went after him" (Pineda 1969). The finance major Seinsoth, it was reported, handled his own negotiations.

The day after graduating from USC, Seinsoth made the short trip north to Bakersfield, California, where he would play first base for the Single-A Bakersfield Dodgers of the California League. It was a day he knew would someday come, the day when Seinsoth would leave the area where he had been born and reared and where he had risen to become one of the most highly regarded young ballplayers in the country. He would join a team with many now-familiar names, like Tom Paciorek, Steve Yeager, and Ron Cey. And, as he had in Fairbanks and at USC, he would leave his mark and do it quickly, proving to the Dodgers in only a short while that they had made the correct decision in drafting him into their baseball family.

Gaye Gammon's USC junior class photo, 1969 (*Garfield Studio*)

At the USC baseball team's annual end-of-the-season party, held at Rod Dedeaux's Surfside, California, beach getaway, Seinsoth arrived with a new friend. Her name was Gaye Gammon, and the two had met earlier in the year through a mutual acquaintance. Then just a junior, Gammon, from posh San Marino, California, and Seinsoth had begun spending time together in group settings as the baseball season wound down, and they continued the relationship as Seinsoth headed off to Bakersfield to ply his trade with the Dodgers. While Seinsoth was away the two corresponded, and his letters to Gammon provide a rare glimpse into his life as a minor-league ballplayer in Bakersfield, perhaps best known at that time as the home of country singer Buck Owens.

"We met at the Student Union through my college roommate," she recalled. "We met a couple times [there] with a group of friends. The first time we actually went out was the year-end party that Rod Dedeaux had down [near] Seal Beach" (Wagner 2015).

The two enjoyed "a few dates," however, Seinsoth soon departed for Bakersfield, and most of their communication after that was through telephone calls and letters, with Seinsoth's missives penned in an ultra-cursive script that he admitted was difficult to read. On the rare occasions when Seinsoth returned home to Arcadia, the two would get together for short visits. Then Gammon left for Europe with her mother and some friends. Although she was gone for much of that summer, her relationship with Bakersfield's newest celebrity continued through their ongoing correspondence. It seems a paradox—she in historic Sweden, Scotland, and other far corners, and he in Bakersfield, Modesto, and Lodi. Both believed the separation would only be a temporary one.

While in Bakersfield, Seinsoth's attentions were diverted, at least somewhat, as he settled in at 500 H Street, Apt. N with, as he later wrote, two other ballplayers, presumably teammates.

"I have a place to live," Seinsoth wrote Gammon. "It isn't bad—there is a pool, but it gets very hot and the air conditioner doesn't work real well so sometimes it can be pretty uncomfortable" (Seinsoth 1969).

At last, despite the discomfort of life in the bush leagues, a career in professional baseball was getting off the ground, something Seinsoth had dreamed about since boyhood. Although college baseball was competitive and thrilling, minor-league baseball was a whole new experience as well as a means to reaching a lofty pinnacle, one that many strive for but few ever attain. Seinsoth planned to become one of the chosen few to wear a Los Angeles Dodgers uniform, and only his own shortcomings as a ballplayer—if there were any—could stop him.

Sam Lynn Park, home of the Bakersfield Dodgers from 1968 through 1994, was a hitters ballpark. Built in 1941

and closed down in 2016, its dimensions were modest: 328 feet down both lines and a meager 354 feet to dead center field. Seating capacity was only 3,600, and with his power Seinsoth figured to knock plenty of balls into the bleachers before his playing days there were through.

Seinsoth's new life officially began on Monday, June 9, 1969—his first day with the Bakersfield Dodgers. He shared the news in a letter to Gammon:

> **Last Monday was something else. I went down to the stadium at 9:30 [a.m.] and I signed [paperwork] at about 9:45. By the time I finished signing and filling out this form and that form, and talked with Don LeJohn, the manager here in Bakersfield, it was nearly 12:00. Then, they had to take pictures—so I got home about 1:00 [p.m.]. Bakersfield played a doubleheader against Reno that night in Bakersfield and I played in both games. In order to get up here [to Bakersfield] I had to move it. I stopped off to say goodbye to my mom but I didn't see my father 'til they came up yesterday.**
>
> **I have a great schedule. Get up about 9 and sit by the pool 'til 12, then rest or read or whatever until I go to the [ball]park at 5. The games start at 8, and afterward, usually between 10:30 and 11:30, we have probably our biggest meal. Weird hours, but it gives me a great deal of time. I hope to read a lot and have thought about getting my books for [grad school] and knocking them off during the summer (Seinsoth 1969).**

Throughout that summer Seinsoth's schedule wouldn't vary much, except during home stands. He discussed baseball travel in his letter to Gammon:

> **We head out on the road for the next six days—three in Visalia and two in San Jose. Traveling is the only bad part. We have our own bus, but it is still eight or nine hours to Reno and far to Lodi, Stockton and San Jose. We will play a game at night and drive all night to play the next night in another town. [Every] three or four nights it is the same thing all over. You have to love the game (Seinsoth 1969).**

Seinsoth's first appearance at Sam Lynn Park, located at 4009 Chester Avenue, was a highlight of the team's second season playing there, at least for manager LeJohn, however, the home runs didn't come as early or as often as anticipated—not at first anyway. In one respect his debut was an exhilarating one as teammate Larry McDowell took a no-hitter down to the final out before surrendering a single, finishing with a one-hit, 5-1 victory in the nightcap of a doubleheader against the Reno Silver Sox. In the two victories that day, first baseman Seinsoth hit fifth and sixth in the batting order after forcing six-year veteran Joe Dodder, the team's regular first baseman and its leading hitter, into the outfield. He walked, was hit by a pitch, and hit into a double play in the opener and walked, struck out looking and struck out swinging in the second game, an inauspicious start by any yardstick.

His first professional hit came the following game when Seinsoth went 1 for 4 with a single against the Stockton Ports. He was blanked the game after that, going 0 for 2. After his first four games Seinsoth was 1 for 9 and searching for answers. An 0 for 3 game on June 13 and a 1 for 4 performance on June 14 left him 2 for 16 and hitting .125.

Seinsoth finally collected his first extra-base hit and RBI on June 15, going 1 for 4 and driving in two runs. Then, on June 16 it was goose eggs again—1 for 4— prompting Seinsoth to write his girlfriend about a new fret he was enduring, something players from rookie ball on up through the major-league ranks still experience no matter what their salary:

Well, it has taken a week, but I am finally getting settled. Things were kind of hectic last week and a lot of things slipped by without my noticing them— including the way I played. I don't think I've ever gotten off to a worse start in my career, [and] after tonight I think I am 3 for 24. Not exactly outstanding for the money they gave me (Seinsoth 1969).

Three for twenty-four left him hitting just .125, not quite the batting average that the Dodgers had envisioned when they signed him. Seinsoth was worn out from a grueling Pac-8 Conference schedule. He was new to the rigors of professional baseball, and it's unlikely that anyone in the Dodgers organization was too concerned about his slow start. No one except, perhaps, Seinsoth.

His mild lamentation proved to be good therapy for Seinsoth, and the next day he went 2 for 4 in a win over Visalia. The game after that he went 3 for 5, belting his first professional home run, a solo shot, and adding a pair of singles in another win over Visalia, raising his batting average to .242—modest but still good considering he was at .125 just seventy-two hours earlier. A week later his 3 for 3 performance in a victory over Fresno, bringing his hitting streak to nine games, further boosted his confidence as well as his batting average (.333 on the season, .485 during the streak) and perhaps convinced Seinsoth he was in Bakersfield to stay—at least until the season ended and the Dodgers promoted him to a higher level of competition.

Following a game against Fresno, Seinsoth inadvertently hinted that the beaning he suffered against Oregon State may have had lasting effects. When a sliding Fresno runner inadvertently kicked him in the head, the trainer, hoping to test Seinsoth's responses, held a finger in front of his eyes. "I told him that wasn't necessary," Seinsoth later said. "I had double vision anyway" (Wagner 1991). The fastball to his eye apparently had taken its toll.

Despite that inconvenience, the low minor leagues and all that playing Single-A baseball entailed were his to endure for as long as he had to. He didn't mind—as he had written to Gammon, "You have to love the game." As the season progressed, there was little doubt about one thing: Bill Seinsoth loved the game. He would love baseball until the bitter, painful end.

11

PINNACLE

"I thought he was a good player. Obviously, he had a future. You could see that he was going to have an opportunity to play in the major leagues."
–Ron Cey, former infielder for the Los Angeles Dodgers, Chicago Cubs and Oakland Athletics

Seinsoth's ten-game hitting streak came to a halt in a June 28 game against the Modesto Reds when he failed to get a hit in three at bats. During the hot streak he had raised his batting average from .125 to well over .300 and had more than proven his worth as a hitter. The second half of the season—for better or for worse—would be much different for the eager rookie. His batting average would drop sharply, although his home-run count would increase measurably. Up until that point he had hit just one round tripper, and he probably felt a little discouraged. A new contract with Hillerich & Bradsby, makers of famed Louisville Slugger bats, had to perk him up, just like a similar contract had to thrill Bill Sr. when he signed with the bat company in 1936. The young man wrote about the agreement, which paid him in sporting goods, in a letter to Gammon, dated July 3, 1969:

I signed a contract with Hillerich and Bradsby and for payment they are sending me a set of golf clubs—10 irons, four woods and a bag. They make bats and they now have the right to use my name—autograph—on the

bats they make. If I start practicing maybe I'll be half decent by the time I get home (Seinsoth 1969).

Seinsoth showed his sense of humor later on in the same correspondence: "My parents are coming up tonight to see the game and then go with us up to Lodi, where we play this weekend," he said. "My dad bought a new Chrysler New Yorker, so they are going to take it on a shakedown cruise. It's not a bad car if you like driving the Queen Mary around town" (Seinsoth 1969).

The next day, July 4, Seinsoth belted a home run against Lodi, and the following week he came back with a first-inning solo blast over the short center-field fence in a game against the San Jose Bees in Bakersfield; he also doubled and singled in the game. A week after that he drove in three more runs with a homer and a single in a win over Modesto. He hit another home run three days later against Reno and still another on August 2 against the Visalia Mets. While his multiple-hit games were trailing off slightly, the hits he *was* getting counted for much: he was, clearly, on a home run tear, prompting the *Tribune* to declare in a headline: "Seinsoth Parking Them Out" (1969). The home runs aside, he described to Gammon in an August 14 letter the bleak scenario of playing in hot, dusty Central California towns:

We are in Modesto, but by the time you get this we will probably be in Bakersfield for our last home stand. This has got to be the worst town in the whole league. Tomorrow, I plan to see two Walt Disney movies at the theater next door . . . Weather has been continued hot with clear skies, but the humidity is getting me down. Still is 95 degrees at 9 p.m. Am certainly looking forward to winter months. I may be back in the heat again, however, if I play in the Instructional League in Arizona instead of going to school. Depends on the [military] draft.

By the end of August, Seinsoth's batting average had dipped below the .300 mark. With ten home runs now in the bank, manager LeJohn inexplicably pulled him from the starting lineup for the final week of the season. While Seinsoth's mother said the move was designed to showcase players who hadn't seen as much playing time as her son had, a letter dated August 19 may more accurately explain LeJohn's decision just as Seinsoth's first season was coming to a close:

> **Well, 16 games left and the end brings mixed reactions. Since the first of the month I've been playing better, but I'm really tired, too. I got hit by a pitch last week, just above the wrist. Then, last weekend I jammed the wrist and had to miss two games—the first I haven't played in since I came here. Sure was nice to get a little rest.**

Seinsoth's final start of the 1969 season came on August 28 as Bakersfield closed out its home schedule against San Jose, and he made his presence felt. He went 2 for 3 with a home run as the Dodgers knocked off the Bees 13-7. His final appearance in a Dodgers uniform, as a pinch hitter, occurred September 1 in a loss at Reno. Seinsoth failed to get a hit in his only time at bat and did not play on September 2 or in the team's finale the following day, replaced at first base by Dodder—who hit two of his three home runs on the season in two nights down the stretch in Seinsoth's absence. For Bill Seinsoth and the rest of the Bakersfield Dodgers, the season was over. They finished a disappointing sixth in the California League standings with a 67-73 overall record.

All in all, Bill Seinsoth's first season in the minor leagues was a success. He had arrived in Bakersfield after the season was well under way, weary but eager to play. After slumping early on he had pulled things together and ended up with acceptable numbers. On top of his final .276 batting average and a more-than-respectable ten home runs, he had eighty-one hits, fourteen doubles, and two triples, driving in thirty-seven runs and scoring forty seven times in only eighty games. Always aggressive at the plate, he was hit by pitches seven times—nearly twice as often as any other player —and he walked thirty-two times, one fewer than the team leader. In his shortened season, Seinsoth had earned his team's respect as an assertive offensive player, someone whose presence at the plate was always worth a private sigh of relief—especially when a game was on the line. He was certainly a clutch hitter in every sense of the term, and the Los Angeles Dodgers considered him a man to contend with if anyone else had designs on becoming the team's regular first baseman after Parker's retirement.

Seinsoth chases a wide throw at first base for the Bakersfield Dodgers, 1969

"He had a great attitude, a great make-up," recalled former Dodgers scouting director Wade. "And, we knew he would only get better." Wade added, "Everywhere he went he hit. He typified the spirit of the Dodgers" (Wagner 1991).

Ever modest despite his outward confidence, Seinsoth wasn't one to bask in his own accomplishments. He playfully belittled himself in a letter to Gammon about a final interview he had granted to the *Bakersfield Californian*. The article was published on August 23, 1969 —twelve days before Seinsoth left Bakersfield and headed home for the winter, a solstice that tragically never came.

"The paper is going to do a feature article on me, so the [reporter] is supposed to come over this afternoon," he wrote. "How can they want to write about a .250 hitter? If he's coming by I should clean the place up a little" (Seinsoth 1969).

Cleaning up was nothing new for Bill Seinsoth. For nearly a decade he had "cleaned up" at ballparks from

Arcadia, California, to Omaha, Nebraska. Now, with his first season in the minor leagues completed, there were non-baseball matters to consider. Seinsoth was hopeful of entering graduate school at USC in the fall, pursuing an advanced degree in finance, and he planned to investigate the possibility of filling an opening in a plum Nevada National Guard unit as a means of fulfilling his military obligation. There was much to do before the Arizona Instructional League would begin, too, something the Dodgers likely would have required he participate in, and as he looked ahead to the 1970 baseball season, there was cause for optimism. Success, as always, was Seinsoth's to grasp, and he was excited about what lay before him. With his baseball future brighter than ever, he had to believe that 1970 would be a very good year. He could hardly wait to make the drive to California, where his family, his new girlfriend, and any number of good things awaited him—including cooler weather. The past year had been a very good one, but even better things lay ahead, he reasoned. He was sadly mistaken.

12

END OF THE ROAD

"The life of a baseball player doesn't last too long."
¬Jane Seinsoth, mother of Bill Seinsoth

The drive from Reno, Nevada, to Bakersfield is a dogleg, cutting west along Interstate 80 before reaching a conjunction with State Route 99 at Sacramento, with SR 99 then dipping due south. It's also a long drive—roughly 420 miles, or at least eight hours according to an estimate Seinsoth himself painted for Gammon in a June 16, 1969, letter. Along the route are several towns that hosted teams Seinsoth had played against, places like Modesto, Visalia, and Lodi, and the trip would have been a familiar one to any California League ballplayer. In anticipation of avoiding the long detour to Bakersfield after the season ended, Seinsoth drove to Reno for the final games, planning to make the exit to Las Vegas afterward a direct one. His parents were also on hand for the season-ending games.

After recently signing the Hillerich & Bradsby contract, Seinsoth stowed in his Volkswagen a carton of bats emblazoned with his autograph. He probably anticipated the Dodgers would elevate him to another level the following season, and therefore he wouldn't be returning in the spring, although it's not known how or when he planned to move his belongings from Bakersfield back down to Arcadia—probably later in the summer. As a

Seinsoth enjoys a lighter moment in the Volkswagen that ultimately cost him his life, c. 1969 (*Seinsoth family photo*)

result of the power he had demonstrated during his shortened stint with the team, a return to Bakersfield and Single-A ball the following season was unlikely. Instead, the Dodgers' Double-A team in Albuquerque, New Mexico, managed by Del Crandall, was a probable next destination, where teammate and good friend Ron Cey ended up. A call-up to the Dodgers' Triple-A Spokane, Washington, club, where Bakersfield teammate Tom Paciorek played in 1970 under manager Tom Lasorda, or even the major-league club were distinct possibilities if things went well enough during the early going in 1970. On the ball field, things usually went well for Bill Seinsoth.

"We were told he would probably go up to the majors [in 1970]," Mrs. Seinsoth recalled years after her son's death (Wagner 1991).

Due to his car's limited trunk space, Seinsoth at some point stowed the bats on the passenger side floor or on the rear seat; he also brought along with him his guitar. Accompanied by his parents, who left several hours ahead of him in the New Yorker, he headed off toward Las Vegas to meet up with former USC teammate and close friend Shafer, the player who replaced him when an Oregon State fastball took him down early in the 1969 season. The trip to Nevada was more than a social visit. Seinsoth had learned from his coaches of an opening in a National Guard unit, and with the Vietnam War accelerating, he wanted to investigate the possibility of enlisting. Presumably, the Guard would allow him to play baseball while he followed a schedule that enabled him to meet his service obligation, although it is not clear how he planned to fulfill the commitment while playing in Albuquerque or Spokane—either one a possible next destination.

The Seinsoths likely left Reno the morning of September 4, motoring all day down US 95 past the Gabbs Valley Range, the town of Goldfield, and Scotty's Junction before reaching Las Vegas. Seinsoth was driving alone in his own vehicle—something he hadn't anticipated.

He had planned to share the drive with teammate Cey, whom he had met during his Goldpanner days and later played against when Cey was a member of the Washington State University baseball team.

"We hung out together," Cey said. "I was one of the people he knew when he first got [to Bakersfield], and that was one of the reasons." He added, "I thought he was a good player—obviously, he had a future. I liked him, we got along well" (Wagner 2015).

Thanks to Cey's willingness to accompany his friend to Las Vegas and on to Los Angeles, the drive would be much less tedious than if Seinsoth traveled alone, and perhaps the two could share some laughs along the way. At the very least, Cey, who later would star as a third baseman for the Los Angeles Dodgers, could help his friend stay awake during the long drive. Unfortunately, for reasons he could not recollect, Cey bowed out of the arrangement and Seinsoth would set out on the long drive by himself.

"We were supposed to ride back together," Cey confirmed. "I don't know exactly why that didn't happen." He added that he likely canceled days before their planned departure rather than at the last minute.

After arriving in Las Vegas on Thursday afternoon, September 4, Seinsoth may have anticipated a late-morning departure for Arcadia two days later, on Saturday, September 6. One scenario had him arriving in Los Angeles early enough to pick up Gammon at Los Angeles International Airport following her arrival from Europe and later watching his good friend, O. J. Simpson, play in his final pre-season football game at

A smiling, relaxed Bill Seinsoth, probably near the end of his life, 1969

the Los Angeles Memorial Coliseum. Simpson would make his National Football League debut the following Sunday, September 14, and Seinsoth didn't want to miss his final warm-up game against the hometown Los Angeles Rams.

As expected, Seinsoth's stay in Las Vegas was a short one, and little is known about his itinerary once he arrived in there. He did bunk at the Dunes Hotel, a now-demolished casino that Shafer's father, Lenny, co-owned. Since September 5 was a Friday, he may have met with the National Guard commanding officer either in the morning or sometime during the afternoon.

Once in town, the evening was his and his parents' to enjoy as they wished, perhaps trying their luck at the town's infamous slot machines, walking the streets along the glittery Strip, or relaxing in the comfort of the Dunes before catching some needed shuteye. Shafer confirmed that on the final morning of their visit, Saturday, September 6, his friend enjoyed a late breakfast with Shafer's father before heading across the Nevada/California desert on newly constructed Interstate 15 toward Los Angeles at about 11:00 a.m., his bats, guitar, and other possessions in tow. Whether his belated breakfast resulted from staying up late and sleeping in is not known, however, his mission for that day was clear: he would swing by the home of his sister, Janice, and pick up two tickets to the Rams-Buffalo Bills game before possibly heading to the airport for Gammon. With Cey unable to accompany him, he may have planned to attend the game with her. Seinsoth would then enjoy a relaxing evening of football, probably under a hazy Los Angeles summer sky. He was eager to watch Simpson play the game that had brought him fame as college football's Heisman Trophy winner in 1968, and there was talk among Seinsoth's family that the young man might also present Gammon with an engagement ring that evening. Unbeknownst to Seinsoth, also planning to attend the game that night was former college roommate and fraternity brother John Bruce.

As dusk falls, the Mojave Desert is a symphony of silhouettes, with native flora and distant mountains punctuating the barren landscape. During the warm daylight hours, drivers along Interstate 15 find little relief from the seemingly endless road tedium except, perhaps, an occasional twist, turn, or change in elevation along the miles and miles of baking highway leading toward Yermo, a town dubbed "Gateway to the Calicos" that is situated near the base of the Calico Mountains east of Barstow. The desert is a panorama of flatland as far as the eye can see, a drowsiness activator for ataractic motorists, and the strong winds that sweep across the hot asphalt make the lonely stretch of highway that Seinsoth would pass through exceedingly dangerous.

After stopping for gas on the outskirts of Las Vegas, National Guard enlistment papers firmly in hand, Seinsoth headed for home and what he anticipated would be a busy day and evening following the 3 1/2-hour, 250-mile drive. The first hours of his journey from Las Vegas would have been uneventful as he passed an occasional desert town or service station and little else of note. Probably near the town of Baker, which today boasts—and for good reason—the world's tallest thermometer, a car pulled onto the highway and began trailing behind him. Having other cars close at hand on a trek across the desert, where an overheated vehicle can result in death, would have comforted him, and if Seinsoth noticed the vehicle in his rear-view mirror, he probably felt relieved at having company, even though he didn't know who the occupants were.

What happened next has never been determined with complete certainty. As Seinsoth's car approached windy Yermo at around 2:00 p.m., his vehicle, which was traveling within the speed limit, inexplicably veered to the left and overturned multiple times, ejecting Seinsoth, whose seat belt apparently broke, through the passenger-side door. Despite suffering critical head and spinal cord injuries, Seinsoth's great strength enabled him to drag himself toward the edge of the roadway and out of traffic before collapsing not far from his car, which had been a high school graduation present from his parents.

The car that had followed behind Seinsoth for nearly seventy miles immediately pulled over, and a man rushed to his aid while a second man proceeded a half mile to a gas station to summon medical assistance. As the roadside drama unfolded, the parents of Craig Perkins, a teammate of Seinsoth on the 1969 USC team, passed by the accident scene, unaware that it involved the former Trojan first baseman, Mrs. Seinsoth once recalled.

The California Highway Patrol long ago destroyed records of the accident as a matter of course, and details of the crash as well as any conclusions the agency may have drawn are obscured by the cataract of time.

However, officers speculated that Seinsoth may have fallen asleep at the wheel before drifting onto the center shoulder, perhaps waking when he felt the ground beneath him become unstable or bumpy and flipping the vehicle six times as he tried to correct his course. Another theory suggests that wind gusts in the area may have pushed him off the roadway, resulting in the same conclusion or even causing the car to roll immediately as a burst broadsided it. A more recent theory also has been accredited: the beaning Seinsoth had suffered in April and the injury to his head, including double vision he experienced into his Bakersfield playing days, may have somehow impaired him as he approached the turnoff to Lake Dolores, causing the deadly accident. Although she believed her son's double vision had disappeared, Seinsoth's mother noted: "We don't know whether the blood clot was cleared up [before the accident]." It was also theorized that the carton of baseball bats he had stopped in Bakersfield to retrieve, bats with the name "Seinsoth" burned onto them, may have struck him in the head as the car overturned, causing the fatal head injuries.

"I will always think that the wind literally flipped his car and he was thrown out—that's it," (Gammon) Farr said. "It doesn't have to be complicated. That's the way I'm going to remember it" (Wagner 2015).

Friend and former USC teammate Shafer shared her conjecture. "It can get pretty windy. I've probably driven that road a thousand times, and you can get a gust of wind and it moves you" (Wagner 2015).

According to Seinsoth's mother, her son tried to speak with his rescuers, but his words were not discernible, and he soon drifted into unconsciousness. Cardiopulmonary resuscitation was performed until rescue personnel were able to arrive and rush Seinsoth first to a nearby Marine Corps logistics base infirmary, then another seventy miles to San Bernardino Community Hospital where more advanced treatment for his traumatic injuries was available. At around dinnertime the telephone rang at the

Seinsoth home in Arcadia, where his sister, Janice, had repeatedly called her parents—Bill Sr. and Jane had departed from Las Vegas some time before their son had and arrived home well ahead of his anticipated due time— to find out why her brother had not picked up the Rams tickets. This time, a nurse was calling to report the tragic news to Seinsoth's parents: their son had been badly injured in an automobile accident. His prognosis was grave.

Family members rushed to the hospital, only to find that Seinsoth was being kept alive by life-support technology. At that point there was little that doctors could do, and at 8:30 p.m. the Seinsoths were ushered into a physician's office and told their son had suffered irreparable brain damage and that all hope was gone. "Oh, no," Mrs. Seinsoth exclaimed, rising from her chair. Moments later, the couple was taken in to see their son, who had no visible marks on him, Mrs. Seinsoth recalled. Seinsoth was then transferred by ambulance to Harbor General Hospital in Torrance, where, in a final selfless act, his kidneys and corneas were removed for transplantation. One kidney was transplanted into James Weirnicz, a thirty-five-year-old father who lived in Costa Mesa, California, and the other into fifty-seven-year-old Jasper Williams of Rayville, Louisiana, who had been using an artificial kidney during the previous year. As Seinsoth's parents hurried to the hospital, Seinsoth's close high school and college friend Bill Caldwell, the last person to see him alive, stood in the hallway as Harbor General staff transported him away on a gurney for the final time.

Gammon learned of the accident when she stopped by her parents' San Marino home after landing at Los Angeles International Airport, where Seinsoth, whom she had hoped would pick her up, was nowhere in sight. Instead, she drove home with others in her travel entourage.

The boyfriend of one of Gammon's travel companions had received word of the crash through USC friends and started a chain of communication that eventually reached her parents, who sent her older sister to bring Gammon from her apartment to their home. "My dad was really upset," she said. "He told me [Bill] had been in an accident, and I said, 'Where is he—I'll go?' [My parents] said he was gone" (Wagner 2015).

Others learned about the accident in very different ways. Dedeaux heard about it on the radio. Arnold's parents telephoned him in Hawaii. A tearful Bill Sr. called his son's high school coach, Exton, to report the tragedy. Exton in turn called Seinsoth's high school teammate and close friend, Dawney. USC teammate Jaffe was at home in Los Angeles when the phone rang, and seconds later his girlfriend—now his wife—ran into the room, exclaiming, "Bill Seinsoth just got into a terrible accident" (Wagner 2015). College roommate Bruce, who had attended the Rams-Bills game at the Coliseum as Seinsoth had planned to do, returned to his girlfriend's home and was watching television when Seinsoth's photo appeared on the screen, a reporter noting that the slugger had been seriously injured. Shenk was hosting a college party in South Pasadena when a woman appeared at the top of the stairs to call out the bad news. He and several friends left immediately for Harbor General Hospital, where they peeked into Seinsoth's room and were able to see him one last time before surgeons whisked him away.

His door was slightly ajar and I saw him, Shenk said. That was the end.

His father was destroyed when Bill died in that car accident. Losing Bill was everything. His father was an outgoing, robust, fun guy—he was one of the guys and a delight to be around. Once Bill was killed he lost his spirit. He definitely lived his life through his son, and when his son was gone he really had no purpose to live (Wagner 2015).

Others also were deeply affected. Dennis Mulhaupt, a young fan when Seinsoth died and the cousin of former Seinsoth girlfriend Janet Mulhaupt, called his death "shattering."

"It would be hard to overemphasize how much I worshipped him," said Mulhaupt, who was fourteen when Seinsoth died. "He was always amazingly nice to me, a young kid who was often annoyingly around and in the way. He always had time for me, was interested in me, and his death was absolutely shattering for all of us." He added, "What a fantastic guy" (Wagner 2015).

On Seinsoth's final night, while he was losing his life in a Torrance hospital, his good friend O. J. Simpson's Buffalo Bills were losing to the Rams 50-20 at the Coliseum in a game he had planned to attend. Simpson, a running back, ran the ball seven times that evening for only twenty yards. The following Sunday, the day after Seinsoth's funeral, Simpson made his professional football debut. Perhaps affected by his friend's death, he rushed for only thirty-five yards.

Well after midnight, with the Seinsoths' ordeal having reached the worst possible denouement, doctors urged family members to return home and get some rest. They complied. While driving home after her son's organs were removed, Seinsoth's mother turned on the car radio. A broadcaster was reporting that Bill Seinsoth was dead.

Mrs. Seinsoth recalled years later that the doctor who removed her son's organs was the brother-in-law of a young man who had worked as a batboy with Seinsoth when he was younger. A year after her son's death, while attending a Los Angeles Dodgers game, she overheard a nearby fan remark following a missed play that "if Bill Seinsoth had been here he would have caught the ball" (Wagner 1991). She turned around to see the surgeon who had harvested her son's kidneys seated behind her.

Seinsoth's death was reported in newspapers from Cumberland, Maryland, to El Paso, Texas, to Corona, California, and points in between, and the European edition of *Stars and Stripes* even covered the story. Perhaps most affected by the tragedy were the communities of Arcadia and Bakersfield, where Seinsoth truly left his mark. In an article matter-of-factly headlined "Bill Seinsoth Killed in Auto Accident," one reporter wrote:

> **The brilliant baseball future of Arcadian Bill Seinsoth, 22, came to a tragic end Sunday when he died after being fatally injured in an automobile accident (Bill Seinsoth Killed 1969).**

The writer went on to describe Seinsoth as a "coveted" ballplayer, perhaps the most coveted in years. "Though there were no witnesses to the accident, a California Highway Patrol spokesman said the former USC Trojan star apparently lost control of his car, which overturned and ejected him" (Bill Seinsoth Killed 1969).

Arcadia Tribune columnist Pineda had followed Seinsoth's career as his star was rising, reporting on his baseball exploits, injuries, or other events in his life—anything that readers might find interesting—with regularity, and he appeared to be affected by the tragedy. Pineda's emotions were evident in a moving column published three days after the player's death, when wounds inflicted upon the community were still fresh. The columnist lamented:

> **Everyone who loves sports in Arcadia is deeply saddened today by the tragic death of young Bill Seinsoth, who died as a result of injuries sustained when his speeding vehicle [sic] apparently overturned. It has ended the promising baseball future of the first baseman owned by the Los Angeles Dodgers. Arcadians are shocked and still can't believe that this young man should be cut down before having the chance to live.**
>
> **His father dreamed of the day when his son would be performing in the major leagues. Nobody doubted for a second that young Bill would make the grade. So**

many Arcadians have followed his exploits since his Little League baseball days here that they felt they had a guiding hand in molding his career . . . (Pineda 1969).

In the days that followed, family members focused their energy on Bill Jr.'s funeral, presenting a service that reflected both his brilliant life and his successful pursuit of the sport he loved—baseball. The 1:00 p.m. service, held on September 13, 1969, and attended by 600 people, was conducted at Arcadia Presbyterian Church and officiated by The Rev. James Hagelganz, the family's pastor. More than 200 cars lined Alice Street and neighboring avenues.

"It was packed," said Hagelganz, now eight-six. "The sanctuary was filled to capacity. I remember standing up in the pulpit and looking out over the audience and seeing the people out there in the packed sanctuary.

"He was such a young guy with such a phenomenal body to be able to accomplish all [the] things that he was able to accomplish" (Wagner 2015).

When the service ended, the lid to Seinsoth's casket was closed, and the coffin was moved from the front of the sanctuary to the narthex, where it was opened for viewing. As mourners exited, teammates and former teammates dropped gloves, baseballs, and bats into the coffin. His sister Dauna, unaware that the casket would be opened and overcome by the finality of seeing her deceased brother, embraced him. Refusing to let go, she had to be pulled away.

"I grabbed him and wouldn't let go," she said. "I was almost lifting him up." She added, "They had to pull me off of my brother" (Wagner 2015).

Attending the church service were a vast collection of ballplayers, including high school friend, Dawney, USC teammate and then-future San Francisco Giant, Barr, Bakersfield Dodgers ballplayers, and representatives of the Los Angeles Dodgers, who delivered a large floral arrangement in the shape and colors of the team logo.

Luminaries included USC coach Rod Dedeaux and then-Dodger Hutton (whose father, a likable Dodger Stadium usher who was Seinsoth's uncle, was later struck and killed by an automobile). An estimated 650 cards were received by the family, including one from Ronald Reagan, who was then the governor of California. In lieu of flowers, the Seinsoth family requested that contributions be made to the Bill Seinsoth Memorial Baseball Scholarship Fund at USC.

While the service was a celebration of Seinsoth's life, there were aspects that saddened the soul. "It was open casket," said Shafer, one of the last friends to see Seinsoth before the accident. "Two bats and a baseball [and Seinsoth's glove] were in the casket" (Wagner 2015).

There may have been something else in the casket. (Gammon) Farr said that during the viewing she slipped a private note and some pressed forget-me-nots inside Seinsoth's suit jacket. The act may have made the ordeal a little easier for her, however, for Shafer he still bears scars of that day.

"That's the last time I looked in an open casket," he said. "I won't do it [again]. It was very, very sad" (Wagner 2015).

When asked the significance of two bats placed atop Seinsoth's chest, Shafer said, matter-of-factly: "They were crossed." Seinsoth's hands were at his sides, according to former USC roommate Bruce, who lived with him during Seinsoth's junior year.

"I remember [offering] condolences to his mom and dad, and they weren't hearing anything," Bruce said. "They were so devastated."

So was Justin Dedeaux, who recalls the lugubrious essence that permeated the church where Seinsoth's memorial service was held and still feels his loss nearly half a century later. "I still cringe when I think about it," he said. "Grief. There was so much grief in that church. I think about it all the time. I remember how devastated everyone was."

Including Bill Sr., Dedeaux said. "I can still see him weeping."

IN MEMORY OF

WILLIAM R. SEINSOTH

Native Of
  California

Passed Away
  September 7, 1969

Services Held At
  Arcadia Presbyterian Church
  Arcadia, California
  September 13th at 1:00 P.M.

Officiating
  Rev. James W. Hagelganz

Interment
  Rose Hills Memorial Park

Funeral program compartmentalizes the sad news of Bill Seinsoth's death (*Rose Hills Memorial Park*)

Former USC teammate Shelly Andrens added, "[Seinsoth's death] broke his dad's heart."

Seinsoth's sister was more emphatic. "My dad was destroyed," she said. "He didn't really go to church after that. He was angry. He poured himself into that boy, idolizing him." She added that after her brother died, her father never again played semipro baseball.

Hutton called Seinsoth's tragic ending "just devastating to my uncle [Bill]," adding, "I couldn't look at [him during the memorial service]."

While he wasn't able to attend the funeral due to his minor-league baseball commitment, former big leaguer Tom House has not forgotten his good friend, who served as a groomsman at his wedding.

"I think about him all the time," said House, who also played with Seinsoth as a member of the Alaska Goldpanners summer baseball team. House described his friend as "a man-child out of high school."

"He was one of my best friends. He was physically intimidating, but a big old puppy dog. Really a nice, nice kid."

Goldpanner teammate Boone also missed the service, but for another reason: his friend's death simply hit him too hard. "Hard enough that I did not go to the funeral," he said. "That would have been real tough for me" (Wagner 2015).

A graveside burial service was held later that afternoon at Rose Hills Memorial Park in Whittier, California, where another baseball star, former New York Yankee Bob Meusel, also is buried. Seinsoth was laid to rest in a plum spot beneath a shady, spreading tree, which, to the chagrin of Seinsoth's parents, later died. When the last tear had been shed and family members and close friends had departed the cemetery for the thirty-minute drive back to Arcadia or to their respective communities, a feeling of grief and emptiness had to overwhelm many of those in attendance, as it does when someone with immense promise is taken away too soon. Not only had the Seinsoths lost a son, uncle, nephew, or friend, but the Single-A Bakersfield Dodgers and possibly the Dodgers' Double-A Albuquerque and Triple-A Spokane affiliates— the latter managed by Dedeaux's good friend, Tommy Lasorda—had lost a likely star first baseman of the future.

"We talked about [Seinsoth]," Lasorda said, referring to Dedeaux. "He was a good ballplayer. He had talent and he certainly would have improved as he went along."

Lasorda, who played against Bill Sr. in the minor leagues, added, "I can't think of any shortcomings [Bill Jr. had]." When asked whether Seinsoth might have eventually become the Dodgers' regular first baseman, Lasorda said, "That sounds reasonable, without a doubt. He had power, he could do everything" (Wagner 2015).

That day, with mourners standing in shared disbelief, the sprawling cemetery, with its lush, green, rolling hills and breathtaking view of downtown Los Angeles, where Seinsoth had hoped to play baseball for the Dodgers someday, added to its legion of grave markers. His epitaph, set not far from where his parents and grandparents were later buried, reads, simply: *In Memory of William R. Seinsoth, A Great Trojan.*

In the world of college sports, there are few higher compliments than to earn the moniker "great Trojan," and Seinsoth deserved the tribute. In the annals of USC baseball, there have been few finer Trojans and few better first basemen wearing cardinal and gold. Since 1947— ironically, the year of Seinsoth's birth—when the College World Series first began, only one Trojan first baseman has won the Most Outstanding Player award: Seinsoth. Only six other first sackers have won the award in the seventy-year history of the tournament. Maybe that's why Dedeaux long ago remarked that any all-time all-USC team that he might select would have to include Bill Seinsoth, whom he clearly considered a great Trojan.

Of all the writers who covered Seinsoth, few did so with more objectivity, admiration, and heart than *Arcadia Tribune* columnist Pineda. That's not a criticism, but an observation. When a writer sees only good in a ballplayer —there never was anything bad to write about Seinsoth— it's difficult *not* to be an admirer. Pineda, who cut his teeth as a reporter during the Great Depression and, thus, recognized negativity when he saw it, may have been a closet fan of Seinsoth, about whom he—like other scribes—found only positive things to write.

Perhaps Pineda hit the mark in a column that touched the hearts of *Arcadia Tribune* readers only days after the big first baseman died. Pineda wrote in a fitting farewell to Bill Seinsoth, a young man cut down by tragedy in the prime of life and who, in the minds of many, will remain forever colored in Dodger blue: "The Good Lord must have needed a slugging batter on his team" (Pineda 1969).

EPILOGUE

"One thing you know more than anyone is how much better the world is because your son passed this way. You have every reason to be proud of him."

–Ronald Reagan, former president of the United States

After Seinsoth's death the family was given lifetime passes to all Los Angeles Dodgers games, demonstrating that the team had no intention of separating from the young man's parents and sisters. On the day after his funeral, USC established the Bill Seinsoth Memorial Baseball Scholarship Fund, which was reported by columnist Pineda. The fund was designated to provide scholarships for baseball prospects in need of financial aid.

On June 19, 1970, the Alaska Goldpanners, describing Seinsoth as a popular player, designated their annual Midnight Sun Game, which was played that year against the University of Arizona, the "Bill Seinsoth Memorial Game" (Seinsoth Night 1970). The game, marred by poor weather, raised a disappointing $545 for the USC scholarship fund. "The Goldpanners are happy to contribute to a fund in the name of such an outstanding individual as Bill Seinsoth," General Manager Don Dennis, father of current GM Todd Dennis, said at the time. "We were only disappointed in that we had bad weather for the special gate, which cut down considerably on attendance" (Money Raised for Seinsoth 1970).

In October of 1969, a month after Seinsoth's death, the Arcadia Board of Education approved creation of two bronze plaques, which were donated by the Arcadia High

Arcadia High's Bill Seinsoth Memorial Award still hangs prominently in the school gymnasium (*S.K. Wagner*)

School Booster's Club. Unveiled on May 20, 1970, the Bill Seinsoth Memorial Award remains affixed to the north wall inside the school gymnasium for all to see and continues to honor the school's top athlete each year, as it has since 1970 when Reid Gunnell was named the first recipient. In helping to introduce the award during the school's 1970 spring sports banquet, Mrs. Seinsoth told the assemblage: "Bill was a very humble boy. We were fortunate to have had him for our son. He always accepted his awards modestly" (Gunnell Awarded Honors 1970). Dave Anderson, Mrs. Seinsoth's grandson and Bill Jr.'s nephew, earned the award in 1976.

On June 21, 1973, the Goldpanners again dedicated the receipts from their Midnight Sun Game to the Seinsoth Scholarship Fund, and on that night Seinsoth's parents were in attendance. Appropriately, Bill Sr. threw out the first pitch as the Goldpanners prepared to play Brigham Young University.

"He was a perfect example of the gentle giant," then-GM Don Dennis said. "He could be as mean as ever on the field, but he'd give you the shirt off his back anyplace else. He was as great a competitor as has ever played with the Goldpanners" (Game Dedicated to Memory 1973).

Wall outside the Arcadia High School field house underscores the legacy of Bill Seinsoth (*S.K. Wagner*)

In July 1973 the Goldpanners announced their all-time all-star team, and Seinsoth was voted the greatest first baseman in the history of that elite baseball organization. Seven former, current, or future major-league ballplayers were elected by fans to the twelve-man squad, including Boone, Dave Winfield, Graig Nettles, and USC teammate Strom.

Also in 1973, the Bill Seinsoth Award, which each year recognizes the highest batting average on the USC team, was established. One of the early winners of that award, in 1975, was fellow Arcadia High graduate Steve Kemp.

In 2005, Seinsoth was named to the USC Athletic Hall of Fame, along with former NFL star Lynn Swann, fourteen-time NFL Pro Bowl player Bruce Matthews, and five-time Pro Bowl selection Clay Matthews Jr. The Matthews brothers are also from Arcadia.

"Bill Seinsoth, whose promising pro baseball career was tragically cut short when he was killed in a car crash at age twenty-two, was an all-American and the MVP of the College World Series for USC's 1968 national champions," his Hall of Fame biography read. "The three-year [1967-69] letterman first baseman had a career batting average of .337. In 1969 he hit .368 with fourteen home runs and fifty-two RBI. He then played in the Dodgers' minor-league system, where he appeared headed to eventual stardom" (2005 Inductees for USC 2004).

Finally, on March 21, 2015, the Arcadia High School baseball program held a fiftieth anniversary celebration in honor of the team's 1965 CIF championship—still the only baseball title in the school's history. Although best friend and teammate Dawney attended, noticeably absent was Bill Seinsoth, whose presence on the mound, at first base and at the plate that season made the coveted championship possible—and served as a steppingstone to what many believe would have been a long and successful major-league career. Nonetheless, the evening was a celebration of Seinsoth's many high school and other achievements, and the school paid him the ultimate honor by officially retiring his uniform, number 20, with a gathered throng of family and fans in attendance.

In January 1969, Seinsoth began dating co-ed Janet Mulhaupt. In an interview forty-five years later, the woman, who became Seinsoth's steady girlfriend, called him "very purpose driven." She said Seinsoth's purpose was to become a big-league ballplayer and that she learned early on what everybody who saw him play eventually realized: his long-anticipated career was well within reach. He was, in fact, a great prospect. Mulhaupt said she had no sense of that when they first met.

Mulhaupt continued, "I had no idea how great he was as a player (Wagner 2015)."

As a tribute to Seinsoth's staying power, at least in spirit, what current GM Todd Dennis believes may be the slugger's uniform trousers and a ball bearing his autograph unexpectedly were uncovered at the Goldpanner offices in 2014. Meanwhile, Seinsoth's school yearbooks, several scrapbooks bulging with yellowed press clippings and faded black and white photographs, his time-worn maroon and gold high school letterman jacket, the guitar he was transporting when his car overturned—it was not damaged—and other personal belongings remain in boxes at the Arcadia home where

Seinsoth was reared, a home now occupied by a niece and nephew who both attended USC.

The Double-A Spokane Indians, who were managed by Tommy Lasorda and likely would have benefited greatly from Seinsoth's services in 1970, recovered impressively from his absence. First basemen on the roster included Seinsoth's cousin, Hutton, who had seen limited action at the position during two seasons—1966 and 1969—with the major league Dodgers, and Bill Buckner, who moved up to the big club later that season with Seinsoth out of the picture and played first base off and on for seven seasons with the team. Future Dodgers first baseman Steve Garvey, also a member of the Indians and a second-team all-American behind first-team selection Seinsoth, played third base for the team. Even without Seinsoth, the Indians became one of the greatest teams in minor league baseball history, and no wonder.

The Dodgers recovered, too, as major league franchises usually do following unspeakable tragedies. Parker retired in 1972, the first season that Steve Garvey saw limited action at first base for the team, and was replaced sporadically by Buckner; by 1974 Garvey had displaced Buckner altogether and was a regular at the position, slugging twenty-one home runs, driving in 111 RBI, hitting .312, and helping fans ease comfortably into the retirement of their beloved first sacker. Garvey would play first base for the team for ten more seasons, and when he departed to join the San Diego Padres in 1983 he left a gaping hole on the right side of the Dodgers infield.

Bill Seinsoth Sr. worked as a college umpire after his son's death, and among the schools whose ballgames he officiated was USC. However, his heart remained at Arcadia High, although Principal Richard Cordano recalled that the school had no contact with the family after Bill Jr.'s death. Until one day, when Arcadia High had an opening for an equipment manager. A natural

The Big Bill Memorial at Arcadia High conjures memories of Seinsoth's father, a one-time member of the St. Louis Browns (*S.K. Wagner*)

candidate for the position was former major leaguer Bill Seinsoth Sr., who applied.

"I hired [him]," Cordano said. "Bill, Sr., was an icon in the community because of his baseball background" (Wagner 2015).

As equipment manager, Bill Sr.'s job was to purchase uniforms; wash those uniforms after each athletic event; prepare the campus for baseball, basketball, football, and other competitions; and make sure that all of the necessary equipment was on hand for each athletic event.

"It was a big job," Cordano said. "He was more than qualified."

"He was happy as a duck in water [working at Arcadia High School]," [Seinsoth] Frazier said. "That was his place. He loved being around all the athletes" (Wagner 2015).

One of the sports that Bill Sr. oversaw was baseball. One day in 1984, while raking the pitching mound that had launched his son to prep stardom, Big Bill suffered a fatal heart attack. He died early the following morning, on February 3, 1984—two days before his sixty-sixth birthday.

When asked whether he believed that Bill Sr. applied for the equipment manager position for sentimental reasons, Cordano was emphatic. "Absolutely," he said.

Like his son, Bill Sr. is still remembered at Arcadia High. The "Big Bill Memorial," represented by a long-neglected plaque that was created to honor members of the school's baseball hall of fame, hangs forlornly near Giambrone Field within view of a long wall outside the field house that prominently bears his son's name as 1965 CIF player of the year. All the honoree names have disappeared.

Ironically, research for this book uncovered that Bill Sr., like his son, had signed a bat contract with Hillerich & Bradsby in 1936. The company still has the plates for his autograph.

After retiring from coaching in 1986 Rod Dedeaux served as director of baseball at USC. Thirteen years after that, as the twentieth century came to a close, Dedeaux was named "Coach of the Century" by *Baseball America* magazine and the newspaper *Collegiate Baseball*. He had previously been named national "Coach of the Year" six times by the American Baseball Coaches Association, and Coach of the Century was an appropriate honor for a man who did so much to advance the college sport during its formidable years. Dedeaux died on January 5, 2006, at the age of ninety-one—perhaps the most successful coach in college baseball history. Fourteen months later his beloved wife, Helen Louise Jones Dedeaux, also died.

As his coaching career advanced, accolades often drifted in. Perhaps most significant was the university's decision to name its baseball stadium Dedeaux Field when it opened to the public in 1974.

When he died, then-USC president Steven B. Sample offered up a stirring eulogy to the iconoclastic coach: "Rod Dedeaux has been a part of USC for more than seventy years, as an alumnus, as a Trojan parent and as a legendary baseball coach who mentored and inspired generations of young men, both on and off the field. He was beloved by fans, colleagues and other coaches, and he will be greatly missed" (Sample Eulogy 2006).

Aging plaques commemorating the selection of many former players to all-America teams still ring the upper walls at one of Dedeaux's old DART offices, which now serves as an unofficial archive for USC baseball. One of those all-America plaques bears a name that few people remember: Bill Seinsoth.

Seinsoth and O. J. Simpson did not keep in touch following their USC days, and Simpson failed to respond to an interview request. Mired in serious criminal proceedings over the last twenty years, the 1968 Heisman Trophy winner as college football's top player is currently serving nine to thirty-three years at the Lovelock Correctional Center in Nevada for kidnapping and armed robbery.

Jane Seinsoth remained her son's biggest fan until her own death twenty-nine years later, speaking on his behalf and appearing at events memorializing his success. She died on June 17, 1998, at the age of seventy-nine, fourteen years after her husband passed away. In an inadvertent double entendre meant to describe the short average duration of a major-league ballplayer's career, she said, somewhat hauntingly: "The life of a baseball player doesn't last too long . . ." (Wagner 1991).

Despite her brother's prominence, Janice Seinsoth remained largely out of the public eye. According to Dauna, in 2008, on the eve of her fiftieth high school reunion, her sister became seriously ill and was soon incapacitated. She died a month later on February 2, 2009.

Sometime during the summer of 1969 Seinsoth used one of his "Bill Seinsoth" model Louisville Slugger bats to blast a home run, and he gave the timber to a young fan. For forty-four years the fan kept the bat as a remembrance of the slugger—until 2013, when he contacted Seinsoth's sister, the only member of his immediate family still living. The fan indicated that at long last he now believed the bat belonged in the Seinsoth family, and he shipped it to her along with two baseballs autographed by her brother. She graciously accepted the gifts as lasting remembrances of the brother she loved.

After retiring as a ballplayer in 1981, Seinsoth's cousin, Tommy Hutton, joined the Toronto Blue Jays as a color commentator in 1990, leaving the organization in 1996. He then joined the Florida Marlins, now the Miami Marlins, where he worked for nineteen years as a Marlins analyst for Fox Sports Florida. After working seventeen seasons as a professional baseball player, Hutton spent thirty-four years as a baseball broadcaster. He also serves as chairman of the Tommy Hutton Baseball Academy, which is situated not far from his home in Florida.

Born in Mexico in 1908, sportswriter Mannie Pineda was one of the first Mexican-American journalists in the US, and he worked for seventy years as a sportswriter throughout Southern California's San Gabriel Valley. Pineda's career began in 1923 when he was hired as a correspondent for the *Pasadena Post*. After that he worked for the *Pasadena Star-News* from the late 1920s until 1960, leaving there to work for a variety of small newspapers during the 1960s, 1970s, and 1980s, including the *Hollywood Citizen, Azusa Herald, Glendora Press*, and, of course, the *Arcadia Tribune*. A World War II veteran who fought in the Battle of the Bulge, Pineda died of cancer in Rialto, California, at the age of ninety-one in December of 1999—just days before the turn of the century. In dedicating its 1961 Southern California High School Track & Field Record Book to him, the Helms Athletic Foundation in Los Angeles called Pineda, perhaps modestly, "a most capable sports journalist for most of his adult life."

The Rev. James Hagelganz, who officiated at Seinsoth's memorial service and was senior pastor at Arcadia Presbyterian Church when the author was a teen-aged member of the congregation, is alive and well and living near San Diego, California. Now eighty-six, he still recalls with clarity the details of that heartbreaking service.

Nearly fifty years after Seinsoth's death, Richard Cordano, the youth's high school principal and the man who hired Seinsoth's father as equipment manager, suffered a fall at his home just blocks from the Arcadia High School campus and Giambrone Field. On April 23, 2016, he passed away peacefully at the age of ninety-four. Cordano's memory of, and respect for, Arcadia High School's greatest baseball player—and one of its greatest athletes ever—remained as keen as ever up until his own passing.

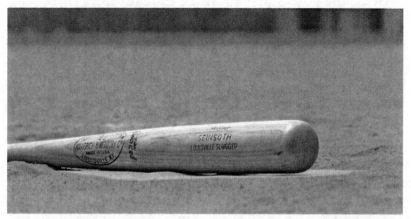

Perhaps the last of Seinsoth's original personalized Louisville Slugger bats, given to friend John Dawney by Seinsoth's parents (*S.K. Wagner*)

AFTERWORD

"Of all the guys I played with I thought [Bill] was going to be on the fastest track to the big leagues of any of them. He could hit, he could field, he could throw and he could pitch. He was definitely a big-league talent."

–Tom House, former pitcher for the Atlanta Braves, Boston Red Sox, and Seattle Mariners

I was just a teen when Bill Seinsoth lost his life, the memory of those long blasts toward Duarte Road only a few months old. I had often wondered how such a perfect hitter could lose his life so imperfectly and incomprehensibly, in broad daylight on a straight and uncongested stretch of Mojave Desert highway in near-perfect weather. A campus slasher couldn't slow his trajectory—neither could a fastball to the eye. Authorities theorized that the accident occurred after he simply made a mistake and fell asleep at the wheel, but I found that explanation simplistic. Seinsoth, a perfectionist, didn't make mistakes, not big ones, and there had to be more to explain his death, as USC teammate and good friend Shafer also seemed to believe.

Hoping to better understand Seinsoth's tragic death, many years later I drove the same stretch of Interstate 15 from Las Vegas to Los Angeles, a 181-mile strip of highway where more than 1,000 people died in automobile accidents between 1994 and 2008 alone (Hargrove 2010). I got more than I bargained for—and a hint of what some believe may actually have occurred on September 6, 1969.

Bill Seinsoth, 1969

As I approached Yermo a strong wind gust blew my car halfway into the fast lane and toward the center of the road, much the way authorities believe Seinsoth's car also may have been blown before rolling over. Although I quickly regained control of the vehicle and continued on, I realized how a strong wind gust might easily have overturned a smaller vehicle such as Seinsoth's Volkswagen.

"Windy, isn't it?" my wife asked, rhetorically.

The next moment, a loud explosion in the right rear tire sent the car thumping and swerving. Fearing the vehicle might flip, I tapped the brake pedal intermittently, coming to a stop on the right shoulder of the highway. I took a deep breath, then looked to my right and spotted a billboard pointing the direction to Lake Dolores. Seinsoth's Volkswagen, a much smaller vehicle that I now believe could easily have blown over, had overturned at precisely that location. Standing on the spot where Seinsoth had used his home-run-hitting strength to crawl toward the edge of the roadway, I examined the torn tire—understanding how quickly an uneventful drive can turn nasty and glad to be alive.

Suddenly, everything made sense.

ACKNOWLEDGMENTS

"Bill was a terrific player. [He] had great hands [and] great power. He was awfully good."
–Bob Boone, former infielder and catcher for the Philadelphia Phillies, California Angeles, and Kansas City Royals

When I started this project it became clear early on that capturing the essence of a beloved Trojan, a "terrific player," as former big leaguer Bob Boone put it, would require significant assistance from the USC family. Throughout the research and writing processes, that assistance was enthusiastically provided.

Justin Dedeaux, son of the great USC coach and chairman of the Trojan Baseball Alumni Association (TBAA), permitted unfettered access to his father's personal baseball scrapbooks, most importantly those encompassing three key years: 1967, 1968, and 1969—Seinsoth's varsity seasons. Jerry Merz, Seinsoth's freshman coach, filled in the missing piece, providing comprehensive information on Seinsoth's freshman season as a Trojan. My thanks to both of these men.

Rachel Caton, assistant sports information director with the USC Athletic Department, provided easy entrée to the USC baseball archives located within Heritage Hall, including original news releases, media guides, and mimeographed stat sheets. When photos were requested, she provided those as well, and sports information director Tim Tessalone readily approved my use of them. I'm grateful to both for their cooperation.

Kenneth Miller, past president of the TBAA, provided contact information for many of Seinsoth's teammates. His assistance proved essential as I attempted to contact players for interviews, including former major leaguers, minor leaguers, and ballplayers who never played baseball professionally. Onetime USC teammate Sheldon Andrens, a member of the TBAA board of directors and a former Seinsoth roommate, filled in historical gaps and provided anecdotes when further information was requested.

The National Collegiate Athletic Association (NCAA) also offered pivotal assistance. J. D. Hamilton, assistant director of media coordination and statistics, made available comprehensive statistical data for every game played during the 1968 College World Series, including USC's five victories. The information allowed me to reconstruct a detailed chronology of Seinsoth's and the team's successes that week as they continued on to win USC's fifth national title.

Ballplayers who competed with Seinsoth at Arcadia High School and USC, along with Alaska Goldpanners and Bakersfield Dodgers teammates, were willing to share with me the sum total of their personal and baseball experiences involving Seinsoth. Without their recollections of events that transpired half a century ago, this book would not have been possible.

Special thanks also goes to Todd Dennis, general manager of the Goldpanners, who provided photographs and statistical data used in this book. His assistance (and an invitation for me to throw out the first pitch before a future Goldpanners game) is greatly appreciated.

The vast majority of statistical information contained on these pages was provided by Baseball-Reference.com. It would be impossible to footnote each citation, and I am grateful to the website for compiling this data. Much of the Seinsoth story was also reconstructed using news accounts from that period, including articles derived from newspapers that long ago closed their doors. As a historical record, there is none better than the Fourth Estate.

A big thank you goes to the Los Angeles Dodgers, not only for drafting and signing Seinsoth, but for helping me connect with a former Dodger great, Seinsoth's long-ago teammate and good friend Ron Cey, who but for an unexpected change of plans would have accompanied his friend on his fateful journey. Team historian Mark Langill put forth my interview request early on in the process and in short order a conversation with Cey, who in 2014 was voted the greatest third baseman in Los Angeles Dodgers history, was arranged. I am grateful.

I am especially thankful to the Seinsoth family, including Dauna (Seinsoth) Frazier, Seinsoth's cousin, Tommy Hutton, nephew Dave Anderson, and niece Deborah Neal for providing key information and photographs, and to Gaye (Gammon) Farr, who was willing to share Seinsoth's personal correspondence with me. The cover photo, provided by Anderson, was expertly restored by Richard Quindry of Richard Quindry Photography. Through the family's assistance and interviews with scores of people, including dozens of former players, coaches, classmates, girlfriends, roommates, fans, clergy, educators, and others, I was able to capture the Seinsoth story in all its athletic glory. For their willingness to discuss their brother, cousin, uncle, friend, boyfriend, student, and teammate, I wish to thank each and every one of them.

Finally, sincere thanks goes to my mother, Mary Lou Wagner, an expert editor who assisted in proofreading this manuscript. Without her meticulous eye, it is certain that typographical and other errors might have gone unnoticed.

Due to the lack of eyewitness corroboration, the fading memories of sources and the absence of various participants in Seinsoth's life, certain logical assumptions, including likely thoughts and actions from long ago, were made. In each instance such actualizations are believed to have occurred based upon the historical record and the author's knowledge of baseball.

In closing, I'd like to offer my special thanks to the late Bill Seinsoth Sr. and his wife, Jane, for sharing their son, if only for a short period. Although his time on Earth was brief, his impact was substantial and significant, and he proffered a lifetime of thrills and enough excitement to fill several books. That's who this project has been about from the beginning: Bill Seinsoth, a baseball legend who might have become a much bigger one had his life not ended so tragically. In light of his many accomplishments while he *was* on this Earth, Bill Seinsoth remains, as Ken Miller put it and as Seinsoth's grave marker affirms, a "great Trojan," someone whose copious persona made writing this book a sincere privilege. —**SKW**

APPENDIX

Bill Seinsoth's final interview, which appeared in the *Bakersfield Californian* on August 23, 1969—fifteen days before his death.

—

Bill Seinsoth Enjoys Baseball Life (Marin 1969)

By Vic Marin

—

You only eat one meal a day. You don't get home from work until 11:30 at night. Doesn't sound like much of a way to live, does it?

However, Bakersfield Dodger first baseman Bill Seinsoth enjoys playing baseball for a living. "The hours are great. You get to the ballpark about 6 and you're finished five hours later. You can sleep all day if you want to and you've got tons of time on your hands during the day. You eat steak every day, too."

Seinsoth, an all-American first baseman at USC in 1968, the Pacific-8's top hitter in 1968 with a .429 average, and the most valuable player in the College World Series admits there are some drawbacks to being a minor-league player.

"We're playing ball when everybody else is off work and having a good time. You can't have conventional dates because most girls work during the day and they usually have to be in by the time you've finished ball.

"Time's the biggest problem. You have to find something to do during the day. You can only do so much of each thing, like reading, watching TV, writing letters, or playing guitar. You try to make everything last a little longer so you won't have any time left before it's time to go to the ballpark.

"The road's even worse since you can't go anywhere and you have only three dollars a day meal money."

College baseball was not a grind the way the minor leagues frequently are, but Bill says, "I like playing every day. I switched to first base in college from pitcher because I wanted to play every day." (He was 15-1 and all-Southern Section CIF as a senior in high school.)

Comparing the minor-league player to college players, he noted that "the quality here is more consistent than it is in college. You face good pitching every day and the pitchers have better sliders. They've mastered their pitches and their control more."

Bill feels the slider has given the pitcher a sharp advantage and attributes his mediocre Dodger average (around .250) to its efficacy and to his being "psychologically worn out after just graduating in June. I need a month's vacation right now."

"College baseball takes a lot more time than most people realize. You're in school and playing or practicing nearly every day."

In college, Bill and [U]SC flew to most of their away games unless they were playing in the Southern California area, whereas the Bakersfield Dodgers travel in a bus on the road.

Big universities also tend to be more generous with food money toward their athletes. Three dollars a day for food on the road isn't much if you're eating anything more than hamburgers and french fries.

College crowds are smaller for the normal, everyday game, but games for titles such as the Pacific-8 championship or the College World Series draw as well as Triple-A.

Seinsoth recalls playing before as many as 5,000 at Pullman, Wash., against Washington State and 10,000 in the 1968 College World Series.

A week-long road trip the week before he took finals at SC didn't help Seinsoth's morale. "I really wasn't too sad when we didn't finish first in the Pacific-8 this year. As it was, I hardly came out of my room during that time right before finals."

"If we'd won the Pac-8 we would have to practice for the College World Series and I wouldn't have been able to catch up in my classes."

Including Bill, nine of the SC players on the 1968 collegiate national champions eventually signed pro contracts.

Bill enjoyed his tenure at SC, because he was one of the best athletes at a school where you're apt to bump heads at any time with such well-known athletes as O. J. Simpson, Mike Garrett, Ron Yary, Steve Sogge, or Bill Hewitt.

"Most of these guys were friends of mine and that's what makes SC such a great school in my mind. The great athletes have really built a tradition at SC.

"I really felt SC did a lot for me. I'm kind of anxious to get back." (He will attend graduate school at SC in finance beginning in mid-September.)

He notes that all the athletes have a great deal of camaraderie. "We all root for each other because we all know each other."

Bill is a great fan and friend of Simpson and believes O. J. should have received more to sign than Lew Alcindor, since he draws larger crowds.

But he recognizes that the merger of the two leagues took care of huge bonuses the same way his baseball draft took care of huge bonuses.

Seinsoth may perhaps be a little anti-Alcindor from the damage Lew did to SC while playing at UCLA. Bill feels SC center Ron Taylor was "badly burned" by the LA press, who were constantly comparing him unfavorably to Alcindor and the Los Angeles Lakers' Wilt Chamberlain. Bill, for one, wasn't too amazed at Taylor's being drafted second by Seattle.

Seinsoth does admit he enjoys basketball as much or more than baseball and one time was offered a combination hoops-baseball scholarship to Arizona State University. "I was a 6-1 1/2, 206-pound forward who couldn't shoot too well but averaged 15 rebounds a game."

Getting back to baseball, the question is whether Seinsoth will start taking baseball as seriously as he took it in college—which he felt was important enough to finish before he signed with the Los Angeles Dodgers this June. He has the natural ability to be a star, but so do most of the players in the minor leagues. College stardom does not mean instant big-league success, as Seinsoth or even O. J. Simpson may learn.

BILL SEINSOTH'S COMPLETE
MINOR-LEAGUE HISTORY

SEASON	TEAM	LEAGUE	LEVEL	AB	BA	H	2B	3B	HR	RBI
1969	BAK	CAL	A	294	.276	81	14	2	10	37

BILL SEINSOTH, SR.'S, COMPLETE MINOR-LEAGUE HISTORY

(BASEBALL-REFERENCE.COM 2014)

SEASON	TEAM	LEAGUE	LEVEL	W	L	ERA
1936	SACRAMENTO	PCL	AA	3	8	5.84
1937	COLUMBUS	SALL	B	15	7	2.74
1937	SACRAMENTO	PCL	AA	0	1	N/A
1938	HOUSTON	TL	A1	9	9	3.59
1938	ROCHESTER	IL	AA	1	0	N/A
1938	COLUMBUS	AA	AA	0	2	N/A
1939	COLUMBUS	SALL	B	17	10	2.41
1940	COLUMBUS	SALL	B	16	10	3.59
1940	ROCHESTER	IL	AA	0	1	N/A
1941	NEW ORLEANS	SOUA	A1	10	11	4.29
1942	NEW ORLEANS	SOUA	A1	24	10	2.79
1943	TOLEDO	AA	AA	9	15	3.40
1944	TOLEDO	AA	AA	16	11	4.08
1945			INACTIVE			
1946	SACRAMENTO	PCL	AAA	0	1	N/A
1947	SAN ANTONIO	TL	AA	5	14	3.17
1948			INACTIVE			
1949	MACON	SALL	A	13	9	2.80
1950	MACON	SALL	A	18	11	2.44

TOTALS:
13 SEASONS   **156**   **130**   **3.22**

BILL SEINSOTH'S CAREER HIGHLIGHTS

Arcadia High School: Champions, California Interscholastic Federation (CIF), Southern Section, Division 4A, 1965

CIF Most Valuable Player, 1965

Selected in the 15th round (296th overall) of the June regular amateur entry draft, Houston Astros, 1965

Signed a letter of intent to play baseball at the University of Southern California (USC), 1965

Selected in the ninth round (155th overall) of the June secondary amateur entry draft, Baltimore Orioles, 1967

Alaska Goldpanners Most Valuable Player, 1967

USC: Champions, National Collegiate Athletic Association (NCAA), 1968

College World Series Most Valuable Player, 1968

Selected in the fifth round (ninety-fifth overall) of the June secondary amateur entry draft, Los Angeles Dodgers, 1968

Selected in the fourth round (seventy-eighth overall) of the January secondary amateur entry draft, Washington Senators, 1969

Named to the American Association of College Baseball Coaches All-America first team, 1968

Named to the Sporting News All-America team

Selected in the first round (eighth overall) of the June
secondary amateur entry draft, Los Angeles Dodgers,
1969

Played one season with the Los Angeles Dodgers' Single-A
affiliate, the Bakersfield Dodgers, 1969.

Named to the USC Athletic Hall of Fame, 2005

BILL SEINSOTH'S STATISTICS DURING THE 1968 COLLEGE WORLD SERIES

(NCAA NATIONAL COLLEGIATE ATHLETIC ASSOCIATION 2014)

OPPONENT	AB	H	R	2B	RBI	HR	BA
BYU	3	1	1	0	0	0	.333
OKLA. ST.	3	0	0	0	0	0	.000
ST. JOHN'S	4	2	0	1	0	0	.500
NC STATE	4	2	0	1	1	0	.500
SOUTH. ILL.	4	2	1	0	2	1	.500
TOT.	**18**	**7**	**2**	**2**	**3**	**1**	**.389**

USC COACH ROD DEDEAUX'S NCAA BASEBALL CHAMPIONSHIPS

1948 (co-coached by Sam Barry), def. Yale
1958, def. Missouri
1961, def. Oklahoma State
1963, def. Arizona
1968, def. Southern Illinois **(MVP Bill Seinsoth)**
1970, def. Florida State
1971, def. Southern Illinois
1972, def. Arizona State
1973, def. Arizona State
1974, def. Miami (Fla.)
1978, def. Arizona State

BILL SEINSOTH'S STATISTICS AT USC

YEAR	AB	H	2B	3B	HR	RBI	BA
1966	52	19	6	1	4	18	.365
1967	171	56	11	0	2	31	.327
1968	138	43	5	0	6	23	.312
1969	174	64	16	3	14	52	.368
TOT.	**535**	**182**	**38**	**4**	**26**	**124**	**.340**

BILL SEINSOTH'S MANY MISFORTUNES

Seinsoth inexplicably falls from the bleachers at a semipro ballpark in Southern California, early 1950s.

Pressure from parents who believed he was too good causes the Seinsoths to pull their son out of the Arcadia National Little League—1958.

Baseball thrown by a semipro pitcher who was warming up nearby strikes the young batboy in the head, causing minor injuries—c. 1960.

After he accidentally spiked a star player, causing him to miss the entire season, pressure forces the Seinsoths to pull their son out of the Arcadia Babe Ruth League—c. 1962.

An unidentified assailant slashes Seinsoth across his pitching hand following an outing at Balboa Island, California, in an incident he rarely discussed—1964.

Batted ball breaks Seinsoth's nose—1964.

Surfboard strikes Seinsoth in the nose, breaking it—1964.

Surfboard again strikes Seinsoth in the nose, breaking it—1964.

A knife-wielding assailant slashes Seinsoth across the forearm in a restaurant near USC, causing considerable blood loss in an incident he again rarely discussed—probably 1967.

Seinsoth's left wrist is broken by a pitched ball causing him to miss a month of games during the championship season—1968.

Fifteen stitches are needed to close a wound caused when a fastball thrown by an Oregon State pitcher strikes Seinsoth's eye, resulting in split vision and a blood clot. Knocked unconscious, he is carried from the field and hospitalized—1969.

Seinsoth is killed when his car rolls over multiple times on Interstate 15 in California's Mojave Desert—1969.

INDEX

7-Up Bottling Co.—8, 32-33, 35

A

Adamson, Mike—12, 71-72, 79, 88, 92,

Alaska Goldpanners—9, 11, 79-80, 83, 97, 105, 118-120, 154, 157-159, 172, 181

Albuquerque Dodgers—142, 143, 155

Alcindor, Lew—177

American Association of College Baseball Coaches—89, 116, 181

American Baseball Coaches Association—163

American League—7, 11-13, 21, 85

Anderson, Dave—158, 173

Andrens, Sheldon—79, 81-82, 154, 172

Arcadia Babe Ruth League—8, 30, 36, 38, 94, 114, 186

Arcadia Board of Education—157

Arcadia Coast Little League—30, 33

Arcadia Community Regional County Park—32

Arcadia Floor Covering—17

Arcadia High School—1-2, 6-10, 12, 30, 33, 39-40, 42-43, 45-46, 48, 50, 52, 55, 57-61, 64, 67, 70, 73-74, 87, 158, 159-163, 167, 172, 181

Arcadia High School Booster's Club—157-158

Arcadia National Little League—2, 17, 32-33, 36, 186

Arcadia Plunge—32

Arcadia Presbyterian Church—8, 32, 45, 152, 166

Arcadia Recreation Department—30, 32

Arcadia Sporting Goods—17

Arcadia Tribune—2, 8, 13, 46, 50, 56, 71, 73, 75, 120, 137, 151, 156, 166

Arcadia Unified School District—28

Arizona Instructional League—140

Arizona State University—58, 62, 178, 184

Arnold, Chris—13, 33, 35, 47, 56, 63-64, 149

Arnold, Jan—102

Athletic Association of Western Universities—95

Atlanta Braves—72, 88, 168

Azusa Herald—166

B

Babe Ruth League—37

Bakersfield Californian—44, 139, 175

Bakersfield Dodgers—ix, 5, 7, 44, 70, 78, 126, 130-133, 135, 138-139, 142-143, 147, 152, 155, 172, 175-176, 182
Baker's Tacos—94-95
Baldwin, Elias J. "Lucky"—31
Ball, Doug—47, 67
Ball, Mike—125
Baltimore Orioles—2, 40, 72, 88, 92, 129, 181
Barr, Jim—12, 78, 91, 96-97, 100, 103, 109, 152
Barry, Sam—66, 184
Baseball America—165, 199
Battle of the Bulge—166
Bellingham Bells—118
Benjamin, Stan—22-23
Big Bill Memorial—162-163
Bill Seinsoth Award—159
Bill Seinsoth Memorial Award—9, 158
Bill Seinsoth Memorial Baseball Scholarship Award—9
Blackwell, Dave—112-113
Blood, Dan—13
Bochte, Bruce—12-13, 47
Boettger, Roger—43
Bond, Jerry—111
Bonds, Barry—79
Boone, Bob—11-12, 79-82, 97, 114, 119-120, 155, 159, 171
Bonneville Salt Flats—18
Boston Red Sox—168
Bostock, Lymon—7
Boucher, H. A. "Red"—79
Bovard Field—60, 67-68, 73, 86, 97-98, 100
Bovard, George F.—67
Braden, Reid—97, 111, 113-114
Brakebush, Steve—47
Breeders Cup—31
Brigham Young University—95, 103, 105, 107, 112, 121, 158, 183
Brooklyn Dodgers—58, 65-66, 68, 70
Brookside Park—83
Bruce, John—145, 149, 153
Bryant, Paul "Bear"—65
Bud Lyndon Swim School—8
Buffalo Bills—145, 150
C
Caldwell, Bill—67, 148
California Angels—7, 91
California Highway Patrol—146, 151
California Interscholastic Federation—ix, 2, 6-7, 33, 39, 47-48, 50-54, 56-57, 59-60, 62-64, 71, 73-74, 85, 87, 115, 160, 163, 176, 181
California League—7, 130-131, 138, 141

California State College, Long Beach—89
California State College, Los Angeles—95, 98, 102
Camino Grove Elementary School—8, 18, 28
Campanis, Al—118, 130
Carroll, Richard—44, 47
Casper, Billy—52
Caton, Rachel—171
Centennial High School—59
Cey, Ron—131, 136, 142-145, 173
Chamberlain, Wilt—177
Chanteurs—45
Chapin, Dwight—99-100
Chapman College—98
Chapman, Ray—7
Chicago Cubs—136
Chicken Delight—8
Cincinnati Reds—81, 105
Clemente, Roberto—7
Cleveland Browns—59
Cleveland Indians—7
College World Series—ix, 2, 7, 13, 58, 75, 96, 100, 102-103, 105-106,
     108, 111, 113-116, 124, 126, 156, 159, 172, 175-177, 181, 183
Collegiate Baseball—163
Columbus Red Birds—20-21, 49, 180
Cordano, Richard—64, 161-163, 166-167
Crandall, Del—142
Crews, Tim—7
Crowley Major League All-Stars—89, 97
Cumberland University—66
Cunerty, Bill—69
D
Dahlgren, Babe—54-55, 62
Dahlgren, Rick—54, 62
Dairyland Farms—17
DART Transportation—106, 163
D'Auria, John—14
Dawney, John—32-33, 35, 37, 45, 50-51, 54, 56-57, 61-63, 67, 73,
     83, 149, 152, 160, 167
Dedeaux Field—164
Dedeaux, Helen—164
Dedeaux, Justin—12, 65, 68-70, 75-76, 83-85, 87, 95, 153, 171
Dedeaux, Rod—ix, 5-6, 12, 14, 19, 58, 65-66, 68-69, 71-72, 75-78,
     84-85, 87-88, 92, 94-95, 97, 99-100, 102-103, 106, 109-113,
     115-118, 120-121, 123-126, 129, 131-132, 149, 153, 155-156,
     163-164, 184
Demolay—32
DeMuth, Bill—4, 9, 41, 62

Dennis, Don—157-158
Dennis, Todd—11, 157, 160, 172
Detroit Tigers—47
Disney, Walt—137
Dodder, Joe—134, 138
Dodger Stadium—xi, 19, 116, 129, 153
Douglas Aircraft—71
Drake, Ron—90, 97, 111, 114
Dunes Hotel—144

E
Earp, Wyatt—31
El Rodeo—69
Evans, Janet—150, 160
Excelsior High School—60
Exton, Lani—12, 19, 39, 41, 47-49, 52-53, 56, 60, 63, 149

F
Fairbanks News-Miner—118-119
Fairly, Ron—128
Fenway Park—16-17
Ferguson, Rich—47, 59
Florida State University—184
Fontana High School—52
Florida Marlins—165
Fox Sports Florida—165
Freshman Baseball Conference of Southern California—72, 74
Fresno Giants—135

G
Gable, Rick—47, 59
Gammon Farr, Gaye—78, 131-133, 135-137, 139, 141, 144-145,
    147-149, 153, 173
Garcia, Vickie—4
Garrett, Mike—177
Garvey, Cyndy—6, 9
Garvey, Steve—5-6, 10, 89, 128, 161
Gehrig, Lou—14, 54
Giambrone Field—2, 42, 60, 64, 163, 167
Gilchrist, Sandy—14, 69
Glendora Press—166
Gunnell, Reid—158
Gwynn, Tony—51

H
Haden, Pat—51
Hagelganz, The Rev. James—45, 152, 166
Hamilton, J. D.—172
Harbor General Hospital—148-149
Hardings Gardenland—17
Harrison, Pat—97, 110, 114, 116

Harvard University—106
Heisman Trophy—97, 145, 164
Helms Athletic Foundation—166
Hendrickson, Joe—106
Heritage Hall—67, 171
Hewitt, Bill—177
High Point University—66
Hillerich & Bradsby—136, 141, 163
Hollywood Citizen—166
Hollywood High School—65
Homik, Bill—110-111
Honolulu Invitational Tournament—99
Hooker, Fair—59
Hostetler, Dave—13
House, Tom—12, 70, 72, 79, 81-82, 88, 95, 154, 168
Houston Astros—2, 6, 13, 63, 75, 84, 92, 129, 181
Hughes, Chad—47
Hull, Mike—69
Hutton, Tom—vii, 2, 5, 21, 26, 55, 128, 153-154, 161, 165-166, 173
J
Jack Murphy Stadium—x
Jaffe, Jay—12, 15, 72, 74, 77, 95, 97-99, 126, 149
Johnny Rosenblatt Stadium—105, 107
Johnson, Randy—66
Johnson, Walter—51
K
Kansas City Royals—171
Kappa Sigma Fraternity—68-69, 78-79
Kay, Bill—48
Kemp, Steve—12, 47, 66, 79, 126, 159
Kennedy, John F.—46
Kingman, Dave—11, 66
Kiraly, Karch—51
Klein, Bob—79
Koufax, Sandy—50, 53
Kuehner, Pat—97, 100, 107-108, 110-114, 124
Kuehner, Tim—107
L
Lake Dolores—147
Lakewood High School—62
Langill, Mark—173
Larkin, Mike—13
Larkin, Pat—13
Lasorda, Tommy—142, 155, 161
Leach, John—48
Lee, Bill—12, 97, 102-103, 108-110, 114
LeJohn, Don—133-134, 138

Lemaster, Denny—6
Little League—ix, 8, 13, 16-18, 33-37, 40-41, 68, 83, 93, 98, 114, 152
Longden Field—17-18
Los Angeles County Arboretum and Botanic Garden—31-32
Los Angeles Dodgers—vii-3, 5-7, 10, 12, 19, 21, 26, 53, 63, 70, 89, 92,
    98, 116, 118, 120, 126, 128-132, 135-136, 139-143, 150-152,
    155, 157, 160-161, 173, 178, 181-182
Los Angeles Dodgers All-Stars—89
Los Angeles International Airport—144, 148
Los Angeles Lakers—177
Los Angeles Memorial Coliseum—144, 149-150
Los Angeles Rams—79, 144-145, 148-150
Louisville Slugger—5, 136, 165, 167
Lovelock Correctional Center—164
Loyola High School—60
Lubbock Christian University—66
Lynn, Fred—66, 85, 126
Lynwood High School—52-54
M
Macon Peaches—28, 29, 180
Marietta College—66
Martin, Billy—7
Marx Tower—68, 72
Matthews, Bruce—159
Matthews, Clay, Jr.—159
Mayfair High School—53
Mayhew, Rob—13
McCombs, Rich—111, 113
McDowell, Larry—134
McGwire, Mark—14, 66
Merz, Jerry—70, 72-73, 85-86, 105, 171
Messersmith, Andy—79
Meusel, Bob—155
Miami Marlins—165
Miller, Kenneth—14, 172, 174
Modesto Reds—136-137
Monday, Rick—79
Monmouth Sun-Enterprise—199
Monrovia High School—49, 59
Montebello High School—43
Montreal Expos—26
Mulhaupt, Dennis—150
Mulhaupt, Janet—150, 160
Mulleavy, Terry—42
Munson, Thurman—7
N
National Baseball Congress—120

National Collegiate Athletic Association—4-7, 19, 65, 84, 94, 102-103, 105-106, 109, 112, 116, 120, 125-126, 172, 181-184
National Football League Pro Bowl—159
National Football League—59, 144
National League—7, 11
Neal, Deborah—173
Nettles, Graig—79, 159
Nettles, Jim—79, 97
Nevada National Guard—140, 143-144, 146
New Orleans Pelicans—21, 180
New York Mets—5, 97
New York Times—199
New York Yankees—7, 23
Noren, Irv—23-24
North Carolina State University—106, 109
O
Oakland Athletics—14, 52, 136
Ohio State University—75
Oklahoma City Oklahoman—199
Oklahoma State University—106, 109, 183-184
Old Scout—75
Olin, Steve—7
Oregon City Enterprise-Courier—199
Oregon State University—7, 89, 122, 135, 143, 186, 199
Owens, Buck—131
P
Pacific Coast League—20
Pacific-8 Conference—44, 95, 100, 115, 120, 129, 176-177
Pacific League—43-44, 46, 49, 51, 59-60
Paciorek, John—199
Paciorek, Tom—126, 129, 131, 142
Parker, Wes—2, 5, 86, 105, 128-130, 139, 161
Pasadena City College—73
Pasadena Independent—73, 106
Pasadena Star-News—130, 166
Pepperdine College—121
Perkins, Craig—120, 146
Philadelphia Phillies—26, 71, 171
Philadelphia Phillies All-Stars—89
Pineda, Mannie—9, 151, 156-157, 166
Pitlock, Skip—112-113
Pittsburgh Pirates—7
Plymouth Elementary School—18
Polo Grounds—16-17
Port, Randy—86-87
Portland Daily Journal of Commerce—199
Powell, Boog—92

Q
Queen Mary—137
Quindry, Richard—173
R
Ramshaw, Chuck—90, 97
Rasmussen, Neil—13
Reagan, Ronald—153, 157
Reno Silver Sox—133-134, 137, 138
Richard Henry Dana, Jr., Junior High School—8
Roach, Stuart—42
Robinson, Jackie—51
Robinson, Vallie—8, 59
Robledo, Fred—9
Rochester Red Wings—21, 180
Rockwell, John—109
Rogodzinski, Mike—111
Rose Hills Memorial Park—10, 154-155
Ruth, Babe—3, 23
S
Sacramento Solons—20, 22, 180
St. John's University—106, 109-110, 183
St. Louis Browns—3, 21, 24, 68, 162
St. Louis Cardinals—20
Sam Lynn Park—132, 134
Sample, Steven B.—164
San Antonio Mission—23, 180
San Bernardino Community Hospital—147
San Fernando Valley State College—121,
San Francisco Giants—13, 33, 35, 63, 72, 91, 105
San Francisco State College—89
San Jose Bees—137-138
San Marino High School—48
Santa Anita Elementary School—8, 32
Santa Anita Little League—30, 33
Santa Anita Park—31
Schaffer, Rich—72, 79
Seattle Mariners—47, 168
Seaver, Tom—11, 66, 79
Seinsoth, Bill, Sr.—vii, 10, 20-24, 26-29, 32, 34-36, 56, 58, 62, 68,
     83-84, 129, 136, 148-149, 153, 155, 158, 162-163
Seinsoth Frazier, Dauna—4, 10, 28-29, 44-45, 51, 83, 152, 165, 173
Seinsoth, Jane—10, 20, 27-28, 141, 148, 164, 174
Seinsoth, Janice—10, 28, 145, 148, 165
Serra High School—52
Shafer, Buzz—69, 71-72, 123, 143-145, 147, 153, 168
Shafer, Lenny—144-145
Shenk, Tom—69, 79, 149

Simpson, O. J.—97, 144-145, 150, 164, 177-178
Smith, Mark—13
Sogge, Steve—96, 177
South Atlantic League—21
Southern Association—21, 24
Southern Illinois University—106, 110, 112, 184
South Pasadena High School—55
Southworth, Jim—109
Spokane Indians—142, 155, 161
Stanford University—89-90, 95, 101, 123
Stars and Stripes—151
Stengel, Casey—65
Stockton Ports—134
Strom, Brent—97, 109, 111, 159
Sumitomo Metal Industries—119
Superior Concrete—17
Suplizio, Sam—81-82
Swann, Lynn—159

T

Tarzan—31
Taylor, Ron—177
Temple City High School—48
The Arcadian—45, 47, 59, 64
The Last Picture Show—39
The Oregonian—199
Times, Los Angeles—9, 12, 199
Toledo Mud Hens—21-22, 180
Torres, Tony—13, 40-41
Trojan Baseball Alumni Association—171

U

United Press International—199
University of Arizona—157, 163
University of Miami—184
University of Minnesota—103
University of Missouri—184
University of Southern California—2-7, 9, 12-14, 30, 33, 44, 58, 60,
    62, 64-75, 71, 77-79, 82, 84-90, 92-100, 102-103, 105-107, 112-
    113, 115-118, 120-122, 125, 127-131, 140, 143, 146-147, 149,
    151-154, 156-157, 159-161, 163-164, 168, 171-172, 175-177,
    181-182, 184-186
University of Southern California Athletic Department—87, 128, 171
University of Southern California Athletic Hall of Fame—159, 182
University of Southern California Medical Center—122
University of Texas—58, 106
University of Washington—89, 101
USC Daily Trojan—4, 69, 72-73, 99-100, 102, 120, 122-123

V
Vaughn, Bob—97, 109
Ventura High School—62
Vietnam War—143
Visalia Mets—135, 137
W
Wade, Ben—ix, 12, 128, 130, 139
Wagner, Mary Lou—173
Ward, Buddy—47
Warren High School—62
Washington Senators—2, 107, 129, 181
Washington State University—89, 102, 122, 125, 143, 176
Wayne, John—51
Way, Warren—43
Weirnicz, James—148
White Memorial Hospital—19
Whittier High School—42, 49, 59
Williams, Jasper—148
Williams, Ted—51, 129
Wilson, Lloyd—7, 122
Winfield, Dave—159
Wooden, John—65
Woods, Tiger—51
Wrigley Field—16-17
Y
Yale College—89, 184
Yakima Indians—118
Yary, Ron—177
Yeager, Steve—131
Yosemite National Park—32
Z
Zamparini, Louis—51

WORKS CITED

"Apaches Collect 10 Hits; Win 5-4." Apr. 7, 1963. *Arcadia (CA) Tribune.*

"Apache Nine Opens Friday against Muir." Feb. 20, 1964. *Arcadia (CA) Tribune.*

"Apaches Tripped 3-2; Bill Seinsoth Fans 13." Mar. 24, 1963. *Arcadia (CA) Tribune.*

Arnold, Jan. "Seinsoth's Goal is Self-Perfection." Apr. 11, 1967. *The (USC) Daily Trojan.* Los Angeles, CA.

Bales, Terry. "Batmen End Trip; to Host Gauchos." *USC Daily Trojan.* Apr. 16, 1968. Los Angeles, CA.

Bales, Terry. "Jim 'Barrs' UCLA from Win." *USC Daily Trojan.* May 7, 1968. Los Angeles, CA.

Baseball-Reference.com. June 12, 2014. http://www.baseball-reference.com.

"Bill Seinsoth Killed in Auto Accident." Sept. 10, 1969. *Arcadia (CA) Tribune.*

"Bill Seinsoth Struck in Face by Surf Board." Aug. 30, 1964. *Arcadia (CA) Tribune.*

Chapin, Dwight. Apr. 19, 1968. "Loss of Seinsoth Weakens Troy Defense, Yet Team Is a Threat." *Los Angeles Times.*

DeMuth, Bill. May 21, 1967. "Seinsoth Back on Top." *Arcadia (CA) Tribune.*

"Don't Forget Young Billy." Feb. 26, 1969. *Arcadia (CA) Tribune.*

"Freshman Baseballers Win Six." Mar. 3, 1966. *USC Daily Trojan* (Los Angeles, CA).

"Game Dedicated to Memory of Late Panner Star Seinsoth." June 21, 1973. *Fairbanks (AK) Daily News-Miner.*

Garcia, Vickie. Mar. 20, 1969. *USC Daily Trojan.* Los Angeles.

Garrett, John. Apr. 1969. "USC's Seinsoth 19-year Veteran."

"Gunnell Awarded Honors." May 24, 1970. *Arcadia (CA) Tribune.*

Hargrove, Thomas. Feb. 26, 2010. "I-15 Stretch Is Deadliest Road in U.S." *Salt Lake City Deseret News (Scripps Howard News Service).*

Jensen, George. June 5, 1965. "Arcadia top Jewel in CIF Diamonds." *Pasadena (CA) Star-News.*

Jensen, George. May 30, 1964. "Lynwood Tops Arcadia, 7-1, for CIF Title." *Pasadena (CA) Independent*: 9.

Marin, Vic. Aug. 23, 1969. "Bill Seinsoth Enjoys Baseball Life." *Bakersfield Californian.*

"Money Raised for Seinsoth Memorial." July 11, 1970. *Fairbanks Daily (AK) News-Miner.*

National Collegiate Athletic Association. July 7, 2014. http://web1.ncaa.org/ncaa/eventlist.do?championship=48&division=4800009.

"No. 1 Star of Trobabes." May 5, 1966. *Arcadia (CA) Tribune.*

"OSU Falls to USC in College World Series." June 13, 1968. *Ada (OK) Evening News.*

Pickard, Don. June 17, 1968. "Another Big Day for Troy." *Pasadena (CA) Independent.*

Pickard, Don. Mar. 11, 1966. "Local Stars Go Collegiate." *Pasadena (CA) Independent.*

Pineda, Mannie. June 11, 1969. "Seinsoth Signs Dodger (Pact)." *Arcadia (CA) Tribune.*

Pineda, Mannie. Sept. 10, 1969. "Sportingly Yours." *Arcadia (CA) Tribune.*

"Punches Fly in Texas Circuit." July 3, 1947. *Miami (Oklahoma) Daily News-Record.*

Roach, Stuart. May 17, 1964. "Apaches Rally, Win 7-6 Play-off in CIF Opener." *Arcadia (CA) Tribune.*

Roach, Stuart. Apr. 11, 1963. "Arcadia Is Third in Pacific Loop." *Arcadia (CA) Tribune.*

Roach, Stuart. June 4, 1964. "Statistics Show Seinsoth Almost Turned the Trick." *Arcadia (CA) Tribune.*

"Seinsoth Baseball Captain." Jan. 9, 1969. *The Daily Trojan.* Los Angeles, CA.

"Seinsoth, Dold Top AHS Hitters." Apr. 8, 1965. *Arcadia (CA) Tribune.*

"Seinsoth Hits College Loop Pitching." Aug. 8, 1965. *Arcadia (CA) Tribune.*

"Seinsoth Key for Arcadia." May 21, 1964. *Pasadena (CA) Independent.*

"Seinsoth Parking Them out." Aug. 3, 1969. *Arcadia (Ca) Tribune.*

"Seinsoth Pitches, Bats Apaches to 4-1 Decision." Apr. 30, 1964. *Arcadia (CA) Tribune.*

"Seinsoth Sharp, AHS Wins, 4-3." May 2, 1963. *Arcadia (CA) Tribune.*

Shadle, Maurice. June 16, 1968. "Kuehner Game-winning Hit Follows Tragedy in Family." *Omaha (NE) Sunday World-Herald.*

"Sportscope: Blood Stays with Three R's." June 23, 1966. *Arcadia (CA) Tribune.*

"Sportscope: The Old Scout." June 9, 1966. *Arcadia (CA) Tribune.*

"Sportscope: The Old Scout." Aug. 4, 1966. *Arcadia (CA) Tribune.* 9.

Swegles, Fred. Apr. 25, 1969. "Batmen Make Traditional Trip North." *The Daily Trojan* Los Angeles, CA.

The Daily Trojan Apr. 23, 1969. "Seinsoth Sees Trojan Win." Los Angeles, CA.

"Trojans' Comeback Fight Earns Praise." June 17, 1968. *Boulder (CO) Daily Camera: Associated Press.*

Wagner, Steven K. Jan. 7, 1991. "They're Left to Wonder What Might Have Been." *Los Angeles Times*. C-Sports sec. C1-C17.

"Wildcat Defense Buries Arcadia." Jan. 17, 1965. *Arcadia (CA) Tribune*.

ABOUT THE AUTHOR

STEVEN K. WAGNER, author of *Perfect: The Rise and Fall of John Paciorek, Baseball's Greatest One Game Wonder* (2015), has worked as a freelance journalist since 1989. The author began his career with the *Monmouth Sun-Enterprise* in Oregon and later worked for the *Oregon City Enterprise-Courier* and the *Portland Daily Journal of Commerce* before joining *United Press International* as a staff writer and assistant bureau chief in Boise, Idaho. He then worked for the *Portland Oregonian* as the newspaper's Vancouver, Washington, bureau chief and its night crime reporter. Mr. Wagner has freelanced extensively for the *Los Angeles Times*, and his work also has appeared in the *New York Times*, *Seattle Times*, *Oklahoma City Oklahoman*, *Baseball America*, and numerous other newspapers and magazines. A graduate of Oregon State University, he is married and resides in Claremont, California.

CPSIA information can be obtained
at www.ICGtesting.com
Printed in the USA
LVOW10*1910310517

536427LV00010B/15/P